Robert Webber

Other Christian Growth Books:

The Faith-Hardy Christian by Gary L. Harbaugh
Criticizing by William J. Diehm
The Power of Affirming Touch
by Wilson Wayne Grant
A Call to Holy Living by Bruce Larson
Dealing with Your Discontent by Peter L. Steinke

Celebrating
God's
Presence

Christian Growth
B O O K S

Celebrating God's Presence

A GUIDE TO CHRISTIAN MEDITATION

William E. Hulme

AUGSBURG Publishing House • Minneapolis

CELEBRATING GOD'S PRESENCE
A Guide to Christian Meditation

Scripture quotations unless otherwise noted are from the Revised Standard Version of the Bible, copyright 1946, 1952, and 1971 by the Division of Christian Education of the National Council of Churches.

Scripture quotations marked TEV are from The Good News Bible, Today's English Version, copyright 1966, 1971, 1976 by American Bible Society. Used by permission.

Scripture quotations marked NIV are from the Holy Bible: New International Version. Copyright 1978 by the New York International Bible Society. Used by permission of Zondervan Bible Publishers.

Scripture quotations marked KJV are from the (Authorized) King James Version.

Scripture quotations marked NKJV are from *The Holy Bible, New King James Version* copyright © 1979, 1980, 1982 Thomas Nelson, Inc.

Library of Congress Cataloging-in-Publication Data

Hulme, William Edward, 1920–
  Celebrating God's presence.

  1. Meditation—Christianity. I. Title.
BV4813.H57   1988   248.3'4   88-902
ISBN 0-8066-2306-3

Manufactured in the U.S.A.   APH 10-1013

1   2   3   4   5   6   7   8   9   0   1   2   3   4   5   6   7   8   9

Contents

Editor's Foreword

Christian life—like all life—is dynamic. It has direction and involves growth. "Instead, by speaking the truth in a spirit of love, we must grow up in every way to Christ, who is the head" (Eph. 4:15 TEV). God *calls* us to grow. "Grow in the grace and knowledge of our Lord and Savior Jesus Christ" (2 Peter 3:18 NIV). We grow in what God has given us—the grace of being in a relationship with him.

Christian growth is both personal and corporate. Living in interdependence with others, we grow within the Christian community—the body of Christ. This growth is the work of the Holy Spirit. Paul spelled it out clearly: "The fruit of the Spirit is love, joy, peace, patience, kindness, goodness, faithfulness, gentleness and self-control" (Gal. 5:22 NIV).

Although the analogy is from nature's growth from blossom to fruit, Christian growth is not completed in our lifetime. We are always moving, but never arriving. Actually we grow in our *awareness* of our need for growth. And Christian growth may not be as observable to the senses as is nature's fruit. It is patterned after the crucifixion and resurrection of Christ. The experience is seldom steady and gradual. The way *up* may be the way *down*. The new comes out of the death of the old.

Christian growth is therefore a venture of faith that focuses on forgiveness. It happens in response to God's call and is secured only by God's grace.

God calls us to grow by creating within us a desire for it. "As a deer longs for a stream of cool water, so I long for you, O God" (Ps. 42:1 TEV). Peter also described this desire: "Crave pure spiritual milk, so that by it you may grow up in your salvation, now that you have tasted that the Lord is good" (1 Peter 2:2 NIV). Jesus described it as "hungering and thirsting." "Blessed are those who hunger and thirst for righteousness, for they will be filled" (Matt. 5:6 NIV).

The books in this series are intended as helps in this pilgrimage of growth. Each one deals with a particular facet of this adventure. Growth takes place in interaction with the human community. It involves not only our relationship with God but also our relationship with people. Prayer is at the very heart of the Christian life. This book is devoted to a specific kind of prayer, namely, prayer as meditation. As the author, I endeavor to show that meditation has its own unique tradition within the Judeo-Christian heritage. Meditation emphasizes the listening phase of prayer, with the Word of God as the focus for listening. It is holistic prayer in that it utilizes body, mind, and spirit.

As a listening "activity," meditation is a way of receiving for our Christian growth. Besides being a dialog with God, meditation is also a conditioning exercise which the Spirit of God can use for our spiritual development.

Since the ups and downs of our emotions interfere with

the concentration needed for meditation, I describe cathartic prayer as a way of expressing these emotions prior to meditation. The book concludes with a specific format for meditation, which may serve as a guide for initiating this discipline into your life.

WILLIAM E. HULME

Preface

"As newborn babes, desire the sincere milk of the word, that ye may grow thereby; If so be ye have tasted that the Lord is gracious" (1 Peter 2:2-3a KJV).*

These words from the letter of 1 Peter sound similar to Psalm 42: "As the hart panteth after the water brooks, so panteth my soul after thee, O God. My soul thirsteth for God, for the living God" (vv. 1-2a KJV).

When we have tasted the graciousness of God, we naturally want more. We long for it. We develop a thirst, an appetite for it. We desire more of *God*, of the "sincere milk" of God's Word.

The Word of God is like the milk for which an infant yearns at its mother's breast. Because we know God through the Word, the Word is compared to nourishment for our soul. Yet it is *God* who is the object of our longing.

Meditation is a way of receiving the Word. Consequently it is a way of celebrating God's presence. Meditation can *grow* on us because it is a means for receiving the nourishing milk which we need for our spiritual maturity. As we know

---

*The KJV is justified in translating the Greek word *logikon* as "of the word," since it is of the same root as *logos*, which is translated in this letter, as in other books of the New Testament, as "the word." (See the *Interpreter's Bible*, vol. 12, p. 106.)

God through the Word, we mature in our relationship with God, whose graciousness we have tasted.

God has created us to be in communion with God, and our longings are fulfilled when we experience this communion. Through meditation we deepen our awareness of God's presence and realize that we are really never alone.

God's presence rubs off on us. Its influence is shown in the strengthening of our *eyes of faith*. Through these eyes we "see" God when distress and disappointment would otherwise hide God from us. The eyes of faith are able to perceive the light when all else appears only as darkness.

Being aware of God's presence in the present moment brings with it God's gift of serenity—the peace described in the Bible as that which "passes all understanding" (Phil. 4:7). It is a peace that fluctuates with the ups and downs of daily living. Yet even in its ebb and flow it provides a genuine foretaste of this peace which will be in its fullness in life eternal.

In its focus on the Word, meditation combines both sides of our communion's conversation—both listening and speaking. Through meditation on the Word we expose ourselves to the Spirit of God speaking through the Word who, "bearing witness with our spirit" (Rom. 8:16), enables us to grow into the kind of person to which God is calling us.

It is through the Spirit's influence in our lives that Christ is formed in us (Gal. 4:19). For Christ is our maturity. The apostle Paul sums it up: "[God] is the source of your life in Christ Jesus, whom God made our wisdom, our righteousness and sanctification and redemption" (1 Cor. 1:30).

Meditation takes us to our Source, who is made known to us in Jesus.

Part One

Meditation as a Form of Prayer

1

Varieties of Meditation

When you think of meditation, what goes through your mind? Transcendental Meditation? Zen Buddhism? An antidote to hypertension?

If I would have asked this question 30 years ago, the answer would probably have been different. Then it would have been *thinking quietly* or *praying silently*. This is because those to whom I would have asked the question would likely have been thinking of the word from the context of their Judeo-Christian heritage.

But in recent years other approaches to meditation have made a major impact in the American culture. As a result, our former awareness of meditation has dimmed.

Changes in our understanding of meditation

Due to this impact of other forms of meditation in recent years, we perceive the word *meditation* differently. For one thing, it has become associated with Eastern religions. Transcendental Meditation is an example of meditation associated at least in its origins with the Hindu religion, Zen meditation with the Buddhist religion, and Yoga also with the Hindu religion.

Through their meditative practices Eastern religions have become more a part of American pluralism than in the past. In fact, it is these influences that have heightened the interest in meditation in our culture. One example of this influence in my own Midwest is Maharishi University in Fairfield, Iowa, founded for the furtherance of Transcendental Meditation. It was formerly Parsons College, a college related to the Presbyterian Church USA.

Meditation has also become *secularized*. Medical science finds this secular approach to meditation useful. Dr. Herbert Clarke Benson, a cardiologist on the Harvard Medical School faculty has pioneered the medical use of meditation. Although he began his work with meditation by using Transcendental Meditation, he soon devised his own method based on the word *one* as a symbol of integration, peace, and harmony.

Benson's method is used in some hospitals for cardiac patients and those with hypertension. The tranquility meditation produces is good for both conditions and does not have the undesirable side effects that medications for these conditions may have.

In Fort Worth, Texas, the Simonton Clinic uses meditation for the treatment of cancer patients. Physician Carl Simonton founded this clinic to help people use meditation to support or reinforce their chemotherapy or radiation treatment.

In preparation, the patients are asked to draw one of their cancer cells and one of their healthy cells. Usually the patient draws the cancer cell as strong and formidable and the healthy cell as weak and vulnerable. Actually the opposite is true, for otherwise the chemical would poison the healthy cell rather than the cancer cell.

After having this comparison explained to them, the patients draw their cancer cell as weak and the healthy cell as strong. Using this imagery, they are assisted in a meditation exercise in which they imagine the chemical poisoning their cancer cells and leaving their healthy cells unharmed.

The patients are also helped to "see" the disease-fighting antibodies in their own bodies attack their cancer cells and destroy them.

In the book *Getting Well Again* (O. Carl Simonton, Stephanie Mathews-Simonton, James Creighton [Los Angeles: J. P. Tarcher, Inc., 1978]), Simonton describes the good results of some patients from this supportive meditation, both in living longer and in living qualitatively better lives than control groups that took only the chemotherapy. He has also noted some cases of remission. In those instances of remission where the cancer later was reactivated, Simonton has observed that this activation usually occurred during a period of great personal stress.

Optional use as secular or religious

The Benson and Simonton methods of meditation, devised by physicians, do not depend on meditation as a religious practice, although Christians and those of other religions may use these methods in that way. On the other hand, Transcendental Meditation and Zen and the various yogas can be used by people of no religious belief as well as by Christians, as each puts the practice into their own mental or spiritual context of images.

I took the introductory presentation to Transcendental

Meditation, in my exposure to these other forms of meditation, and also a course in Silva Mind Control. As far as secular meditation was concerned, I preferred the unambiguously secular format of Silva Mind Control. This course of training teaches meditation without calling it such. Stressing a scientific base, the Silva program is presented as a "science of the mind." Interestingly, the Maharishi decided to join his Transcendental Meditation with science, calling it "The Science of Creative Living."

In the Silva program the meditation exercises repeat a verbal ritual comparable to a religious liturgy as a way of "taking" one to the "inner depths of one's mind." The phrase "better and better" is a familiar part of this liturgy, and the ritual itself is frequently referred to as "conditioning."

2

Devotional Meditation

Our purpose in this book is to revive the understanding of meditation that many in our culture had prior to the popular emphasis on meditation in recent decades. The word *meditation* and the practice it denotes have their own unique emphasis in the Judeo-Christian heritage.

Meditation in the Bible

The references to meditation in the Bible describe the practice. For example, "I will meditate on all thy work, and muse on thy mighty deeds" (Ps. 77:12). Here *meditate* is used in parallel with *muse*, and God's work and mighty deeds are the objects under consideration.

Again, "My soul is feasted as with marrow and fat, and my mouth praises thee with joyful lips, when I think of thee upon my bed, and meditate on thee in the watches of the night" (Ps. 63:5-6). Here *meditate* is used in parallel with *think*—with God himself the object of the thought. A church prayer to which we shall refer later asks for "thoughts that pass into prayers."

According to Psalm 63, meditation is a practice one does at night, when one is on watch, and the experience is a feast for the soul.

"O how I love thy law! It is my meditation all the day" (Ps. 119:97). Meditation is also practiced during the day and the law of God is its object. In this old covenant context, the Law of God is synonymous with the Word of God.

The Book of Joshua places the time for meditation in both day and night. "This book of the law shall not depart out of your mouth, but you shall meditate on it day and night" (Josh. 1:8). Again, it is the Word that is the object of meditation.

In line with these biblical descriptions, the Youth Leadership Training Schools of the denomination in which I grew up had a daily place for meditation. Long before we heard of the Maharishi, immediately after lunch we were given Bible verses or prayer suggestions and directed to go by ourselves to meditate on them for an hour.

The Spiritual Life Missions of the U.S. Air Force, in which I took part on several occasions in my early days of ministry, had a similar program of daily meditation.

Response to God's call

I prefer the term "devotional meditation" to distinguish this kind of meditation. It is meditation practiced within the perspective of faith in God and is devoted to God. It is not simply something that one chooses to do, but rather it is one's response to God's call.

In this perspective meditation is a way of praying. The word *devotional* ties meditation to the Christian practice of daily devotions.

Meditation is, as Brother Lawrence said, the practice of the presence of God (Brother Lawrence, *The Practice of the Presence of God* [Grand Rapids: Baker Book House, 1975]). It is a means of becoming aware, increasingly aware, of the presence of God that is with us always. "I am with you always, to the close of the age" (Matt. 28:20b).

The problem is that we lose awareness of God's presence, and often when we most need it. For all practical purposes we can become practicing atheists at such times. In meditating on a daily basis, we are devoting a specific time to being conscious of the presence of God so that we are more likely to retain this awareness at other times.

3

The Listening
Phase of Prayer

In devotional meditation the focus is on the Word of God, as it is recorded in the Scriptures. It is the Word because God speaks through it to us. As we listen to God speak through the Word, we are by this process realizing God's presence. This is prayer as *listening*.

A two-way conversation

If prayer is conversing with God, then it needs to be a two-way conversation. One-way conversations lose the stimulus of dialog. The beginning stage of meditation is the listening phase of this conversation.

The responding phase of prayer in which we direct a message to God is obviously influenced by our prior listening. This applies also to human conversations. As the letter of James says, "Let every man be quick to hear, slow to speak" (1:19). This same wisdom applies also to our prayer conversation.

Since meditation begins with the listening phase of prayer, there is a role in it for silence—the silence of listening.

When the Spirit of God speaks to us through the Word, we pause to listen. In listening we focus our thoughts, slow down the frenetic pace into which our minds can accelerate, and become more open to receive. This is the reason that medical science is interested in meditation. The state of mental serenity that meditation can engender is the opposite of the stress state of mind so injurious to health. Stress—actually *dis*tress—can lower our resistance to disease by inhibiting our immune system.

A health measure

The Christian motivation for meditation is not the same as that of medical science, and, as we noted, meditation does not need to be Christian to fulfill its purpose for medical science. In fact, its secularization is a plus for medicine since it is then applicable to all patients.

Even though health reasons are not basic to a Christian motivation to meditate, the health-producing aspect of meditation is only enhanced by the devotional context of Christian meditation. Not only does it produce the quieting effect on the mind that physicians appreciate; it also provides the support of a relationship. In meditation we are listening to Someone whose power is greater than our own. The mental quietness is based then on trust.

The combination of quietness and trust is described in Isaiah as a source of strength. "In quietness and in trust shall be your strength" (Isa. 30:15).

By positioning us under God, devotional meditation helps us to affirm our identity as God's children. This is quieting to the spirit because it provides us with a sense of control.

We become stressful when it seems our lives are out of control. When we position ourselves under God in meditation, our sense of control returns in the form of trust.

Trust in the Higher Power is the Christian response to our frustration with powerlessness. As we listen to God we can take charge of ourselves—direct ourselves. Because of our trust we can, as the King James Version puts it, possess our souls (Luke 21:19).

4

Holistic Prayer

Meditation is a holistic way of praying since it is based on the interrelationship of body, mind, and spirit. This inter-relationship—emphasized now in medical and related sciences—is an ancient teaching of the Judeo-Christian tradition.

The contrast in Christianity

In fact, when Christianity began expanding into the world of its day, it found itself in conflict with the surrounding cultures which stressed the separation of body from mind and spirit.

In the Greek culture, influenced by the teachings of Plato, meditation was understood as the spirit's "leaving" the body for a spiritual tryst with God in the realm of the spirit. The body, together with material things in general, was considered inferior to the mind and spirit and a hindrance to their proper functioning. The body was commonly described as a "prison house of the soul."

For Plato, the immortality of the spirit was fully realized when its bondage to the body was broken by death so that the spirit could join the realm of the spirit. Can you imagine the reaction when the Christian gospel of the resurrection was proclaimed in the Graeco-Roman world? It was mind blowing to say the least.

But behind this understanding of eternal life was the belief in a Creator God who created all that is, including the body, and saw it as *good* (Gen. 1:25).

In the third century in Persia, Manes developed a system of beliefs that relegated the body even further from the life of the spirit than did Plato. In fact, Manichaeism taught that the physical world was so inferior to the realm of the spirit that God did not create it. Rather a demiurge or secondary deity created it. The supreme God created only the world of the mind and spirit. St. Augustine belonged to this sect before he became a Christian.

The radical difference in the Christian belief regarding the physical world was behind the formulation of the Nicene Creed in the fourth century. Could God be incarnated in a physical body? Was Jesus a real human being—and still divine? "We believe in one Lord Jesus Christ, the only Son of God, eternally begotten of the Father . . . true God from true God. . . . he became incarnate from the virgin Mary and was made man."

The same tension existed also in the understanding of the sacraments. Can the earthly, the physical, the material, be the conveyer of the heavenly, the intangible? Can bread and wine convey the body and blood of Christ? Can water in Baptism be the means for receiving the gospel?

While a great deal is made in our day of the concept of holism—holistic health and holistic healing, for example—

this emphasis is obviously nothing new. Rather, our Western sciences are now recognizing what their Eastern counterparts had affirmed all along. The unity of our personhood is shown in the interrelationship of our body, mind, and spirit.

Interrelationship of body, mind, and spirit

We experience this interrelatedness in many ways. How is your patience, for example, when you have a nagging headache? Or your disposition when your stomach is upset? Our body affects our spirit.

So also the tensions in the spirit affect the body and mind. How long before your head begins to ache or your stomach begins to hurt when you are emotionally upset? How long before your back aches or some other physical symptom occurs when you overextend yourself and feel stressed?

These are warning signals to slow down, to deal with your style of living, to live a balanced life. Those who don't get these physical symptoms when they are tensed in mind and spirit are the less fortunate. Not having the warning signals of pain, they may permit their tension to go unresolved for too long—with severe damage to their bodies.

Pain is a warning signal to get our attention. The diseases most feared are those that do not give these early signals in pain while something can still be done to help the disease.

Where we used to label some illnesses psychosomatic, we now see psychosomatic influences in all physical illnesses. The only question is, to what degree is the total person—including the mind and the spirit—involved in this particular malfunctioning of the body?

Some psychotherapies are built upon this interrelatedness. Bioenergetics, for example, is based on the theory that tensions in our mind and spirit are "buried" as muscle tensions. Relaxing the muscles, then, is a way of getting these buried tensions back into the consciousness where they can be dealt with directly. Bioenergetics has specially designed physical exercises for this purpose.

Rolfing and other forms of deep massage have similar anticipations, namely, that relaxing the muscles of the body will assist in the healing of the total person. If there is considerable pain, for example, from the pressure of the masseur, this could indicate a tensed muscle in which is locked a mental tension.

When I was receiving a deep massage I felt intense pain as the masseur bore down on a particular leg muscle. "Does that hurt?" he asked, noticing my grimaces. When I answered that it did, he asked, "Can you tell me what is going through your mind?" About all that I could tell him was that it reminded me of the excruciating pain I had when having my ears lanced as a child. I believe he was disappointed.

In our day we rely on drugs to reduce our tensions in our stress-related illnesses. Here again the interrelatedness is apparent. A chemical given to the body relaxes the mind.

It was the possible side effects of such drugs as well as their potential addictive quality that led Dr. Benson to experiment with meditation as an alternative relaxer.

With meditation, however, the process is reversed. We use the mind and the spirit to reach the body. Yet the reaction may still be chemical. The way we direct our mind and spirit may affect the biochemistry of our body.

5

The Spirit
in Breathing

Breathing is emphasized in devotional meditation as a holistic way of praying.

The rhythm of breathing

When we are tense in our mind and spirit, we tend to breathe irregularly, which in turn disturbs the harmony of our bodily functioning. We also tend to breathe shallowly—unless we do the opposite and hyperventilate—breathing from the upper part of our lungs rather than from our diaphragm.

One of my professors in seminary advised his students to take 12 slow, deep breaths when they became tense or upset and they would feel better. In so doing they would be reversing their natural tendency to breathe shallowly when tense and instead would be providing their cells with the necessary oxygen. Also, they would be recapturing the natural rhythm of regular breathing, which in itself is relaxing.

In taking a deep breath and exhaling, in restoring rhythm to our breathing, we are encouraging ourselves literally as well as figuratively to become still—so we can know who is God (Ps. 46:10). When we know who God is, we get straight also our own identity as God's creation—God's child. This reassurance of who we are consoles us.

Christianity originated in the Near East and continues to reflect its origins. Even as meditation has been emphasized in our Western world through the increasing presence of Eastern religions, so also the Eastern branch of Christendom is more recognized for its meditative practices than are the Western branches.

Breath as spirit

Among these Eastern Christians are the Hesychasts, an ancient religious order dating from the third century, who devote themselves to meditation. The word *hesychast* is a Greek word meaning "repose."

A Christian breathing exercise is described in the literature of the Hesychasts.

> You know, brother, how do we breathe: we breathe the air in and out. On this is based the life of the body, and on this depends its warmth. So, sitting down in your cell, collect your mind, lead it into the path of the breath, along which the air enters in, constrain it to enter the heart together with the inhaled air, and keep it there. Keep it there, but do not leave it silent and idle; instead give it the following prayer, "Lord Jesus Christ, Son of God, have mercy upon me." (Quoted in Robert E. Ornstein, *The Psychology of Consciousness* [San Francisco: W.H. Freeman, 1972], p. 121).

The last sentence of the quote refers to the Jesus Prayer,

or the Prayer of the Heart, to which we shall refer in Chapters 14 and 23.

The Hesychasts do not use deep breathing in their meditation exercises simply because they are Easterners utilizing a familiar exercise in meditation. They are *Christian* Easterners in whose tradition the word for *breath* and the word for *spirit* are the same. In both Testaments much is made of the identity of these two words (*ruach* in Hebrew and *pneuma* in Greek).

In the creation story, for example, it was only after God *breathed* upon the man whom he had formed from the dust of the earth that he became a living being (Gen. 2:7). Reflecting on this story, theologian Joseph Sittler wrote, "My personhood is of nature (dust of the earth), natural but *enspirited* by the breath of the Creator" (*Gravity and Grace* [Minneapolis: Augsburg, 1986], p. 10, italics mine).

In Ezekiel's vision of the dry bones, Ezekiel is commanded to prophesy that breath shall enter the bones and they shall live. "Behold, I will cause breath [spirit] to enter you, and you shall live" (Ezek. 37:5).

In the New Testament story of the resurrection, the risen Christ appeared to his disciples and availed himself of their ancient tradition of associating breath and spirit. "He breathed [*pneuma* as a verb] on them, and said to them, 'Receive the Holy Spirit' [*pneuma* as a noun]" (John 20:22).

Prior to this, when the Pharisee Nicodemus was told by Jesus that he needed to be born again, Nicodemus was puzzled. How could he enter a second time into his mother's womb and be born? Jesus answered him by again using these interchangeable words. "The wind [*pneuma* as a noun] blows [*pneuma* as a verb] where it wills, and you hear the sound of it, but you do not know whence it comes or whither it goes; so it is with everyone who is born of the Spirit [*pneuma* as a noun]" (John 3:8).

On the day of Pentecost this analogy was powerfully dramatized. Why was the outpouring of the Holy Spirit upon the disciples of Jesus accompanied by the sound of a mighty rushing wind? Because *spirit* and *wind* are the same word! As they were gathered together "a sound came from heaven like the rush of a mighty wind [*pneuma*], and it *filled* all the house where they were sitting. . . . They were all *filled* with the Holy Spirit [*pneuma*]" (Acts 2:2, 4—italics mine).

Everybody there understood the significance of the sound of wind (spirit) filling the house, with the Holy Spirit (breath, wind) filling the people. It is unfortunate that our English translations do not, or cannot, capture this play on words so significant to the holism of the biblical tradition.

Breathing as praying

Soren Kierkegaard compared praying to breathing. "To pray is to breathe," he said, "and the possibilities of prayer are for the self what oxygen is for breathing" (*Sickness unto Death* [Princeton, N.J.: Princeton University Press, 1954] p. 173).

Even as praying is to our spirit what breathing is for our body, so focusing on our breathing in meditation prepares us for prayer. The old hymn captures the imagery.

> *Breathe on me, breath of God;*
> *Fill me with life anew,*
> *That I may love all that you love*
> *And do what you would do.*

6

Compassion in
the Abdomen

The abdominal area is significant for meditation.

The abdominal region is considered in Eastern meditation as the body's center. When I participated in human potential workshops I was exposed to the martial art of Ai-Ki-Do. *Ai-Ki-Do* may be translated as "the way of harmony with the forces and laws of nature." It is based on concentrating on the abdomen. Keeping one's mental focus on this bodily region while engaged in combat is focusing on one's center of gravity.

Our instructor would direct us to imagine a garden hose coming from our abdominal region, bifurcating at our chest with a branch under each forward-extended arm and the nozzles at the finger tips.

We were to "see" the water from this hose splashing against the wall beyond us. Then the instructor would direct our partner to pull or push us off balance. This was very difficult to do. But when he directed us to take our eyes off the wall where the water was splashing and focus on the nozzles at our finger tips, our partners could easily throw us off balance.

Amazing as it may sound to a Westerner, our mental focus has a lot to do with our physical stability. It's hard to pull one off balance whose mental focus is beyond as well as upon one's body. It is as though the mind was reinforcing the pull of gravity to keep us fixed to the earth.

As the center of our body, the abdominal region also serves as a symbol of our spiritual center—the basis for our personal stability and security. "Centering" is an old and familiar term in meditative practice. It means focusing on the source of our being.

In its Christian context this means focusing on our relationship with God in whose image we are created. As we focus our mind on our relationship with God who is both within and beyond us, we become "rooted" and "grounded" in love, as the apostle Paul expressed it (Eph. 3:17). This stabilizes us in our inner conflicts just as focusing on one's abdomen keeps one stable in martial arts.

Symbol of compassion

But the abdominal region has its own particular significance in the Christian tradition. It is the symbol in the Bible for compassion and affection. In fact, it is usually translated as such rather than literally. A typical example is the apostle Paul's greeting to the Philippians. "For God is my witness how I yearn for you all with the affection of Christ Jesus" (Phil. 1:8). The meaning is literally "with the intestines (*splanchna*) of Christ Jesus."

The King James Version is unique in its attempt to preserve the symbolism. In the above verse, for example, the King James reads, "For God is my record, how greatly I long after you all in the bowels of Jesus Christ." At other times this version tried to preserve the holism of the biblical symbol by combining the literal with the symbolic meanings in the phrase, "bowels of compassion" (1 John 3:17).

Actually, *bowels* will hardly do in our day. *Viscera* is not much better. I believe this is where the problem of translation lies; we have no acceptable word to translate *splanchna* correctly. The closest would be *gut*, and we use the word as such, referring to gut level, meaning the feeling level. But *gut* is not a sophisticated word, to say the least, and hence is not used in our translations, even though it is precisely how we colloquially use the term.

Source for intercession

In a symbolic way our prayers of intercession come from our abdominal area, since it is the seat or symbol of compassion and affection.

Jesus' miracles of healing have this origin in his compassion for those who were suffering. "As he [Jesus] went ashore he saw a great throng; and he had compassion on them, and healed their sick" (Matt. 14:14). We could translate this more accurately by saying that "Jesus saw a large crowd, and he was moved in his gut and healed their sick."

Even we Westerners, if asked to place our hand where we feel compassion or affection, will often place it on our abdomen. "Here in the gut," we say.

So in meditation we focus on our abdominal area as a physical setting for our intercessory prayers. We allow ourselves to *feel* (in our gut) our compassion (suffering-with) for sufferers, and proceed from this seat to pray for them.

7

Intercessory Prayer

Has anyone ever told you when you were suffering from physical or mental pain that they were praying for you? How did you respond to this? I imagine you felt less lonely in your pain and more supported.

We need each other

When God created us God decided that it was not good for us to be alone (Gen. 2:18). So God created also human communities to provide the support we need—biological families, friendship families, geographical communities, spiritual communities.

The church is the epitome of these communities because it is the image of Christ's body. As the community of believers—the communion of saints—the church is like the network of members in a physical body. In this analogy Christ is the head, connected with all of the other members of the body like the nervous system connects all bodily parts with the brain. We are also connected with the other members in a support system comparable to the interrelationship of members in a physical body.

One way in which we provide this support is by praying for others. God has chosen to work through our intercessory prayer.

We do not live in isolation; rather we are involved with people for whom we care and who care about us. There are, of course, *down* times in our lives when we question whether anyone really cares whether we live or die. But normally when our depression lifts we see things differently. Our lives are connected with relationships which influence us. We are bonded by them in love.

A network of support

Our love for others helps us identify with them in their needs. We *feel* with them, and so we pray for them.

These prayers provide a network of support which I am only lately growing to value. When I was a young parish pastor our custodian was an elderly man who took a vital interest not only in his work but in me and my ministry. On more than one occasion he told me, "I get up at five in the morning, pastor, and have my prayers. I pray for you every day." My mother also shared with me that she was praying for me.

While I certainly appreciated their interest and prayerful concern, I do not recall actually believing I needed this support. My own efforts and my own prayers were the more important factors. I no longer believe this. In fact, I believe we should let others know of our needs, cares, problems, so that they can pray for us.

There are people in serious trouble because of marriage problems, family problems, health problems, or financial problems who let none of their friends know. When their problem can no longer be hidden, they are frequently asked, "Why didn't you let us know?" The answer is usually, "I didn't want to burden you with it. There was nothing you could do—I was hoping I could work it out myself."

My inner response to these answers is, "Did you not feel any need for my prayers?"

We tend to be more influenced by the American ethos of independence, of keeping our problems to ourselves or at least within the immediate family, than we are by the Christian ethos of interdependence in which each member needs the others for their own proper functioning.

There are times when we can become overwhelmed by the pains of others. News reports of death and devastation, of imprisonment and torture, or war and revenge, can make us feel helpless.

What can we do in the face of all this suffering?

Henri Nouwen says that at these times we need to move from our hands to our heart. Though we cannot do anything tangibly to alleviate such suffering, we can allow ourselves to feel with the sufferers. We can pray for them.

If our sense of helplessness in the face of such troubles were replaced by prayers of intercession, we would be doing something. We would be using a divinely chosen means to assist the sufferer.

But before we can feel with others in their pains we need to feel with our own pains. If we run from these, we will avoid the pains of others. Or as Nouwen puts it, if we feel first with ourselves, we can then let the pains of others into our space.

The connection between identifying with our own pains and with the pains of others is also the connection between praying for ourselves and praying for others.

8

Jesus' Devotional Model

We can learn much about prayer and meditation from the devotional life of our Lord.

Jesus was an Easterner in his earthly sojourn and his prayer habits are difficult for us Westerners to follow. For example, who in our culture would organize a mountain climb to secure a helpful atmosphere for prayer? I am sure that people have done it, but they have not been too public about it because the rationale would be difficult for our Western mindset to understand.

Yet this is the story behind the transfiguration of Jesus. It did not just happen. Jesus prepared for it. He took with him Peter, James, and John and led them up a high mountain to pray (Luke 9:2-29). It was while they were praying on this mountaintop that the transfiguration took place. This is probably the origin of the term "mountain-top" or "peak" experience.

Sanctuaries of nature

In addition to the sanctuaries of the Temple and synagogue Jesus chose the sanctuaries of nature—mountains, "the lonely places," deserts, and gardens. He retreated to these shrines frequently with his disciples to be "apart by themselves."

How did Jesus' enemies know where to find him to arrest him? Judas of course led them, but how did Judas know? The Gospel according to Luke is very clear on this point. Jesus came out of the house where he and his disciples had celebrated the Passover and where Judas had left the group, and "as was his custom" went to the Mount of Olives (Luke 22:39).

When in Jerusalem he repeatedly frequented this shrine of nature in the evening for prayer. On this mountain was the Garden of Gethsemane, which he chose as the setting for his agonizing struggle with God—the kind of prayer which we will discuss in Chapter 18. It was while he was praying in the garden that he was arrested.

He also went to these places by himself to pray. "And in the morning, a great while before day, he rose and went out to a lonely place, and there he prayed" (Mark 1:35). Also he went out at night for prayer and sometimes prayed all night. "In these days he went out to the mountain to pray; and all night he continued in prayer to God" (Luke 6:12).

How can one be ready for the next day not having slept? Obviously Jesus received from prayer the refreshment normally secured by sleep.

Just as obviously his nights of prayer were not a continuous nonstop conversation, but a time of enjoying the relationship with his heavenly Father without needing always to be speaking. He also listened. As an Easterner his nights of prayer were also nights of meditation.

Meditation as rest

There is good news here for those of you who may have difficulty at times in sleeping. It may be helpful to spend those times in prayer and meditation. Focus your mind on Bible passages and parables and stories—and listen. Intercede for the people you know who are enduring difficult times. You may be asleep in a few minutes.

Sleep is a natural process and "trying to go to sleep" may be actually a way of staying awake. When we place our minds on restful thoughts and allow our spirits to be conscious of God's loving presence, sleep can come quickly.

But even if you don't get to sleep, you have rested. The mindset of meditation is quite different from the dreaded loneliness that one often experiences at these times. As a result you will not feel dragged out the next day.

Part Two

Meditation as a Way of Receiving

9

Capacity
for Imagination

Meditation is an exercise of the imagination. Secular meditation has been referred to as "focused imagination" or "visioning" or "imaging." Imagination is the ability to see pictures in our minds.

External sources can stimulate these pictures but we can also decide what pictures to see by using our memories. Imagination is utilized by physicians like Benson and Simonton because we can choose to "see" our body in its various functionings.

We can also "see" ourselves taking this or that action. Because we have the ability to "see" ourselves functioning in specific ways, we have the ability to influence our actual functioning in these ways.

Imagination's negative power

Imagination is a powerful human capacity. Unfortunately, it is often used negatively. When we are frightened, for example, what happens to our imagination? If a member of our family is not home at the expected time we may worry. If the lateness is prolonged we can imagine they were in an accident or even are dead. We are grateful when we find out they are alive—and all right.

The biggest problem with our imagination in this instance is that it creates what usually is needless stress. But under this influence of fear our imagination can do worse—it can block us when we need to move.

The story of the Israelites' failure to enter their promised land is a powerful illustration of inhibiting imagination. They had come out of their bondage in Egypt and through the wilderness accompanied by "mighty signs" of God's providence. But the closer they got to their promised land the more apprehensive they became. Before they attempted to enter they sent in twelve spies to see what the land was like. When they returned, 10 of them reflected the fears of the people. They said that all of the people they saw in the land were giants, and, "we seemed to ourselves like grasshoppers, and so we seemed to them" (Num. 13:32-33).

Is this not what imagination stimulated by fear does to us? Everybody else looks like a giant, and we feel like grasshoppers in comparison, and even believe others see us as grasshoppers also.

The other two spies, Caleb and Joshua, tried to calm the people by saying that the God who led them this far would not fail them now. "Let us go up at once, and occupy it; for we are well able to overcome it" (Num. 13:30).

Have you ever tried to urge someone to go in a direction they feared? How long do you urge before they turn on you in anger? This is what happened to Caleb and Joshua. "Stone these two!" the people of Israel shouted. Anger is often a desperate defense when we are frightened.

So the people refused to enter their promised land and instead wandered in the wilderness for the rest of their lives.

Our imagination can also cause us trouble when it is stimulated by resentment and hostility. We can imagine all kinds of intrigue against ourselves, even "hear" people talking about us. If our imagination is not checked by our return to reason, we can become *paranoid*, which means literally "beyond the mind." In other words, we become convinced that our negative imaginings are true and then imagine ways to retaliate.

What is your imagination like when you are depressed? Doesn't everybody look as bleak and forbidding as you feel? By affecting our way of interpreting what we see and hear, our depressed feelings actually cause us to "see" and "hear" negatively. If we realize in spite of how we feel that our "picturing potential" is out of whack, we can endure these depressed times and come out of them.

But if we begin to believe our negative interpretations, we can sink deeper into the depression.

Imagination's positive power

In devotional meditation the imagination is stimulated by *faith*. Used in a positive way it is just as powerful in the service of faith as it was in the service of fear or resentment or depression.

We use our imagination in listening. It stimulates our involvement.

The language of the Bible evokes our imagination through its use of vivid imagery. We "see" the message. We often say "I see" to mean "I understand." The word for *see* and the word for *know* come from the same root in the Greek of the New Testament.

Jesus' teaching was based on engaging the imagination; he taught in parables. In fact, the Gospel of Mark says that "[Jesus] did not speak to them without a parable" (4:34). A parable is an illustration or mental picture through which the truth is revealed. "If you have faith as a grain of mustard seed, you will say to this mountain, 'Move from here to there,' and it will move" (Matt. 17:20). Can you "see" it move?

10

Asking in Mind Pictures

The imagination is useful in meditation for listening to the Spirit speak to us through the Word; it is also useful in presenting mental pictures as petitions.

Words actually are auditory symbols of mental pictures. If I want to get a picture in my mind into your mind I will use words that will communicate this picture. If you see a different picture, I miscommunicated. If you didn't get any picture, I failed to communicate. What I was saying was probably so uninteresting to you that you began to think of something else.

Petitioning God through meditation

Praying with words is our chief form of responding to God. This is because communicating with words is the chief form of human communication.

Communicating with God in meditation by using only the

mental pictures is a particular way of responding or asking. One is always free even when engaged in meditation to break out into words—to "think" and to "see" the words—to speak them.

At times we may feel more involved if we use words in our prayers. In fact, I like at times to pray aloud. An empty house gives me the opportunity even to shout my prayers or to cry them. This is cathartic prayer, which we will take up later.

But even when I shout it does not mean I am convincing myself that God can hear me better. It's just that in emotional times I feel more involved if I emotionally express my prayers. My sense of communicating is heightened.

Yet there is value to meditation's emphasis on the pictures alone. Symbols, including word symbols, too often become separated from what they symbolize—in this case, the mental pictures. Forms and symbols are necessary for communication and understanding and they enrich both processes, but they can also stifle communication and understanding. There is always the danger of substituting the form for the essence—the symbol for the picture—rather than using them to express the essence and convey the picture.

This same breakdown between word and mental picture can happen also in our asking God for what we desire.

Importance of the picture for faith

Bob was worried about his teenage son. The lad was sullen, rarely spoke to the family on his own initiative, withdrew as soon as possible from the supper table to his room. He frequently returned home very late and would not say where he had been. Bob feared that his son was using drugs and tried unobtrusively to observe the pupils of his eyes.

Knowing that Bob was a devout Christian, I said to him, "I'm sure you are praying for your son."

"I pray for that kid all the time," he said.

"When you pray," I said, "can you see him talking openly to you and the family, cheerful in spirit, not using drugs?"

Bob impulsively drew back from me. "When I think of that boy, all I can see are those sullen eyes."

While I could understand Bob's despair, I wondered whether he could see that his words of asking were not corresponding to the picture in his mind as he prayed them. Instead the picture in his mind was actually the opposite from what his prayer words were representing. It was like Bob was holding one hand out to receive while pushing away with his other hand.

While we must guard against implying that if we don't get what we pray for, it is because we lack faith, the fact is that faith does play a role in our receiving. Jesus said to the blind men asking for their sight, "According to your faith will it be done to you" (Matt. 9:29). Seeing the picture which our prayer is describing is the first step in believing we can receive.

Obviously Bob felt any change in his son was next to impossible and this feeling colored his mental pictures, even when he prayed for this change. Bob would be taking a leap in faith by letting himself "see" in his mind his son behaving in a changed way.

If faith is the milieu of asking, then "seeing" is the milieu of faith.

11

Praying for Oneself

Help me, God! Heal me! Save me! Ease my pain! Guide me! Show me the way! Have you ever prayed these or similar prayers? Probably many times—during periods of stress, desperation, devastation, frustration, illness. Also at times of great opportunity when you desired to do well.

Prayers in great need

We humans are limited, finite beings. We live in continuous uncertainty. We long for the infinite—for security, for certainty. In the press of our extremities we turn to our Creator who is unlimited and eternal.

The prayer of the Breton fisherman says it well: "Lord, thy sea is so large and my boat is so small."

World War II had the aphorism, "There are no atheists in foxholes." Of course there were! But the message was clear. In the foxholes which soldiers dug for protection from shelling, they were conscious of how little control they had over their lives. They could only wait and hope they survived the bombing and strafing. Any illusion of self-sufficiency, of being in control, was quickly dispersed. Intuitively one turned to the Higher Power. "Take care of me, protect me Lord!"

When the disciple Peter attempted to walk on the water toward Jesus, he cried out, "Lord, save me!" as he began to sink into the sea.

We can sink so deeply into our own panic of futility that the only prayer we can articulate is "help!" At times our petition combines with lament and we despair over *ourselves*. "Lord, what's wrong with me?" "How could I be so insensitive, so stupid, so cruel?"

Prayer for ourselves is not confined to times of desperation; we pray for ourselves also in ordinary times. When we are sensitive to reality we know that we are always dependent on God. We cannot even guarantee our life for the immediate future. The old hymn said it for us: "I need thee, O I need thee, Every hour I need thee; O bless me now, my Saviour, I come to thee."

From my own experience it is more like, "I need thee every moment." I need continually to pray for wisdom in making decisions, for maturity in dealing with people, and for the awareness of God's presence when I tend to think only of myself.

Reluctance to pray for self

Some people are reluctant to pray for themselves. Shirley expressed this reluctance by comparing it with asking other people for something for herself. "If I'm asking for somebody else, I can really be persuasive," she said. "But I feel so uncomfortable asking anything for myself that I stumble on my own words. The same thing goes for praying. I feel uncomfortable, even selfish, asking God for anything for myself. But I can really pray passionately for others." Shirley actually felt guilty over "bothering" God about her own concerns.

If those who are reluctant to pray for themselves are men, they are being consistent with the male image of not being dependent. If they are women, they are consistent with the female image of being a nurturer of others.

Usually these people behave similarly in their relationships with people. It is difficult for them to ask anything for themselves, although they can ask for others.

Because of their image of being examples, clergy are often reluctant to seek from others the help they obviously need. In the study of clergy that I and others conducted (*Pastors in Ministry*, by Hulme, Brekke, Behrens [Minneapolis: Augsburg, 1985]) the question was asked, "Are there sufficient resources for counseling for clergy and their families?" The answer was usually *yes*, but often with a qualifier: "How do you get clergy to admit they need the help that is available and to ask for it?"

Since 98% of the clergy in this survey were men, the larger question may be, "How do you get men to admit they need the help that is available and to ask for it?"

If there is a difference between men and women in this regard, this difference may also be a factor in the gender gap regarding religion. According to the Gallup Religion Poll, women place a markedly higher value on religious involvement and participate more in religious activities such as prayer and Bible reading than do men. ("'Gender Gap' Apparent in Survey on Religion," *St. Paul Pioneer Press*, Dec. 13, 1986, by George Gallup Jr. and Jim Castelli, p. 6B). One needs the "Higher Power" when one's own power is not enough.

Humility vs. humiliation

For some of us, to admit we need help would alter our self-image. It would be hard on our pride, our ego. We find it uncomfortable, awkward, to have to ask for ourselves. We know we would be putting ourselves in a vulnerable position. Others could feel superior to us—could even say *no*.

The resistance to ask for ourselves is more often associated with the avoidance of humiliation than it is with humility.

Though these two words sound alike, *humiliation* and *humility* are poles apart. Actually, only the proud can be humiliated. The humble are fully aware of their limits and vulnerability. In fact, it is this awareness that makes them humble. Since they can openly acknowledge their needs, they have little reason to be defensive when these needs are exposed. So when they need help, it is the logic of humility to ask for it.

On the other hand, suppose our security depends on giving others the impression that we have it all together. Then we are vulnerable to humiliation if our vulnerability is exposed.

We hate people who humiliate us because they have attacked our self-respect.

Unfortunately, our self-respect is too often contingent upon concealing our inadequacies. That which is hidden is always in danger of being exposed. But if we are able to live openly with who we are, we are secured by this very openness against humiliation.

If we know God knows us as we are, what is the reluctance to pray for ourselves? Certainly it is not based on the fear of exposure.

Actually it is based on a misconception of humility. It is as though we are making too much of ourselves if we pray for ourselves. Who am I to ask anything for myself? The implication is that I am being selfish—or self-centered—in praying for myself.

A better question would be: Who am I *not* to pray for myself? If I need God's help, what's the big deal in not asking for it?

The only justification for not asking would be if God were offended by our requests. But exactly the opposite is the case. God is offended by our not asking. In our humility we are honest enough to be aware of our limits. And we are not defensive about acknowledging them. So it is natural to turn to God for help.

Who are we to ask God to help us? We are God's own daughters and sons! That in itself is sufficient reason to offer prayers for ourselves.

12

Asking but
Not Receiving

When you were a child it was probably no blow to your ego to ask your parents for help. Nor was it an uncomfortable experience unless, of course, such overtures had been repulsed and rejected in the past.

But would this be the case with our Heavenly Parent?

For some it may not be. What happens, for example, if we pray for something that seems important to us and we don't receive what our prayers had visualized? Is this a rejection of our petition? Of ourselves?

The hurt of rejection

In his delightful autobiography, journalist Russell Baker tells about his painful confrontation with reality at the tender age of five when his father died. "For the first time I thought seriously about God," he recounts. But they were not comforting thoughts. His father had been taken from him suddenly and without warning. "If God could do things like this to people, then God was hateful and I had no more use for him," was the message he gave to the aunt to whom he had been sent for comfort. She tried to console the outraged and wounded child. "God loves us all just like his own children."

"If God loves me why did he make my father die?" the little boy shot back. "That day," Baker wrote, "I decided that God was not entirely to be trusted" (*Growing Up,* by Russell Baker [New York: New American Library, 1982], p. 61).

The key to the little boy's sense of rejection was, "Why did God make my father die?" Little boys, like the rest of us, ask such questions in times of loss because they have been given two seemingly contradictory pictures about God. The one is that he is loving, the other is that he is all powerful. So if bad things happen, a good God made them happen—for a hidden but nevertheless good reason.

Jim, another man who lost a father in childhood, did not know how angry he was at God after his father's death until some years later even though he continued to attend church. While at college a friend suggested that they pray for a mutual friend whose father was very ill. "Why do you want to do that?" he impulsively shot back. He was surprised at the intensity of his reaction. But as he reflected later he realized it was his anger over his own unanswered prayers for his father's recovery that was coming out.

It was to this apparent contradiction the Rabbi Harold Kushner spoke in *When Bad Things Happen to Good People* (New York: Avon Books, 1981). The remarkable response to this book on the part of not only his fellow Jews but also of Christians shows that he voiced their own often unspoken confusion. People were grateful to Kushner that he had the guts to say it openly—bad things do happen to good people. So how does the good God square with this reality?

God in a fallen world

Our prayers are inevitably connected with our mental image of God. If our picture of God contains both the image of power and of love, how do we account for petitions that seem to fall on deaf ears? If God is able and loving, why would he not exert his power to give us what so obviously we need?

The problem in this dilemma lies not so much in our picture of God, as in our unrealistic picture of the kind of world in which we live. This is a fallen world. Things happen in it that are not God's will.

One of the contributors to our dilemma on prayer is the belief that whatever happens is God's will. This belief has more kinship with Islam than with Christianity, with Allah than with Jesus.

It was Jesus who taught us to pray, "Thy will be done on earth, as it is in heaven." We pray this petition because God's will is *not* being done on earth as it is in heaven.

So how does prayer effect any change in the reality of this fallen world?

This question reflects more a Western than an Eastern mindset. We Westerners are scientifically oriented; we want tangible results. If there is an effect, there is a cause. If I pray for healing, for example, and I am healed, then prayer healed me. By the same token, if I am not healed, prayer didn't work.

Once we combine this kind of cause and effect combination with a God of power and love, we are locked into an inevitable conflict with our faith.

For any particular event to occur, many factors or causes, some known to us and some unknown, need not only to be present but also to synchronize in their occurrence. Faith is one of these; prayer for ourselves is another; intercessory prayer is another. Therefore, faith and prayer always help. But since there are also other factors, faith and prayer may not be sufficient to bring about the event.

On the other hand, they may be precisely what is needed to bring about the desired synchronization. So where does this leave God as a cause?

Although all that happens may not be God's will, God is not shut out by such happenings. God can make good use of what he does not will for those open to receive. This is God's *Godness* in a fallen world.

We can always *hope*. The world in which God functions will not always be a fallen world. The "Hallelujah Chorus" of Handel's *Messiah* is the inspiring exultation of this hope. The time is coming when "the kingdoms of this world are become the kingdoms of our Lord and of his Christ, and he shall reign forever and ever" (Rev. 11:15 KJV). But not yet.

13

An Exercise in Responsibility

God has chosen to work through us in bringing change to this fallen world.

Among the chief resources he has given to us for this purpose is prayer. God wants us to ask for what we believe is good. In so doing we not only exercise our relationship with God, but we also function as God's responsible people. Jesus' words, "Ask and it will be given to you" (Matt. 7:7), are based on this connection. The letter of James turns it around: "You do not have, because you do not ask" (James 4:2).

Colaborers with God

Prayers of petition are certainly not our way of pressuring God. If there is any pressure being applied, it is God who pressures us to pray.

Even so, our petitions may not be answered as we envisioned the answer. Yet they are still an influence in the direction of synchronization—ways through which God continues to work.

Is God then dependent on our prayers? If God is the *End*, how can God be dependent on any of his *means*? The fact that God has chosen the means is indicative of this. But having chosen to work through prayer, God *continues* to choose to work through prayer.

In Christian theology, the term "means of grace" refers primarily to the Word as we have it in the Bible and the Sacraments—God's chosen means through which God gives his grace. Prayer, as we have seen, is actually an extension of the Word as a means of grace, through the listening phase of prayer.

The divine purpose in creation is contained in the words, "Let us make man in our image, after our likeness" (Gen. 1:26). The biblical understanding of the image of God is focused on our human capacity for communion with God. God created us in his image as *persons* so God could enjoy a loving relationship with us.

This interaction is the basis for our being God's colaborers (1 Cor. 3:9) with whom God can *collaborate* ("work with"). The apostle Paul describes this collaboration in gardening terms. One sows the seed, and another does the watering. But it is God who gives the growth (1 Cor. 3:5-6). Our prayers of petition are fundamental to our planting and watering.

We are called by God to this co-laboring role. As described by William Sloane Coffin, we are "to help God protect, affirm, and dignify life—more and more of it. . . . God is always trying to make humanity more human, but without us God will not, just as without God we cannot" (*The Courage to Love*, William Sloane Coffin [San Francisco: Harper and Row, 1982], p. 32).

Fulfilling our identity

Prayer—including prayer for ourselves—is a responsibility given to us by our Creator. As created beings we are dependent on our Creator, a dependency we do not grow out of, a dependency that characterizes our identity as human beings. We are most healthy when we recognize our dependency, most realistic when we function as dependent beings. In fact, our maturing could be defined as our continuing growth in this awareness of our dependency. By the same token, illusions of self-sufficiency are the marks of immaturity—of mistaken identity.

Because the awareness of dependency is a mark of maturity, Jesus could point to a child as a model for greatness. It was when his disciples were arguing about who among them was to have the more important positions in the coming kingdom of God. "For he who is least among you all—is the one who is great" (Luke 9:48). This is because a child, the least among us, has no illusions about self-sufficiency. The wisdom of a child is in his or her natural awareness of dependency. If we grow out of this awareness and seek our identity instead in independence, we actually have retrogressed in our growth: we have become less mature than a child.

14

A Way of
Conditioning

When we use meditation as a form of prayer we are engaging in a form of conditioning (the process of repeated experiences that help shape our identity). In this respect we are exercising responsibility for our own development.

We develop as persons through conditioning experiences. We have the basics in our heredity but it takes the environment (conditioning) to develop and shape those basics. We are going to be conditioned by something—many things. The only freedom we have in this conditioning process is in choosing what will condition us.

This freedom comes with growing into adulthood. When we were children we had to depend on our parents or parent substitutes to provide the proper conditioning for our development. When we became adults we assumed this task for ourselves.

But chronological age by itself does not determine adulthood. Adulthood is also determined by our growth into our own identity. In a Christian context, this awareness of who we are depends on our sense of calling under God.

Prayer of the heart

Using our adult freedom to choose our own conditioning is thus a way of choosing our identity, or of responding to our identity. It is a way of exposing ourselves to influences that condition us in the direction in which we are called of God. It is a way of influencing ourselves in becoming the kind of persons we desire to be. The use of the "prayer of the heart" illustrates how meditation is a way of conditioning ourselves.

The expression "prayer of the heart" is from the meditative tradition of the Hesychasts. Henri Nouwen defines the prayer of the heart as the prayer that is most our own—that forms our unique way of reaching out to God (*Reaching Out* [Garden City, NY: Doubleday, 1975] p. 101).

The Way of the Pilgrim, a Hesychast classic which describes one person's search for the prayer of the heart, says that this prayer should be "a short one consisting of a few powerful words" which can be repeated many times. "The mind should be in the heart . . . guiding the heart while it prays" (Robert E. Ornstein, *The Psychology of Consciousness* [San Francisco: W.H. Freeman, 1972], pp. 120-121).

For the Hesychasts the prayer of the heart is the *Kyrie*, "Lord Jesus Christ have mercy upon me." "This prayer," said one of the early Hesychasts, "will teach you everything."

In the Hesychast tradition of meditation, one meditates upon, prays, and otherwise "fills one's being" with the prayer of one's heart. The idea is that if you focus upon the prayer repeatedly in meditation, it will become part of you and you will "hear" it when you most need to pray it (Ornstein).

An example of conditioning

The closest I come to a prayer of the heart is 1 Corinthians 13:4-8. "Love is patient and kind; love is not jealous or boastful; it is not arrogant or rude. Love does not insist on its own way; it is not irritable or resentful; it does not rejoice at wrong, but rejoices in the right. Love bears all things, believes all things, hopes all things, endures all things. Love never ends."

I am a family-oriented person and I realize how important love as described in these words is for family relationships. I also realize that this kind of love is not natural to me—that I need to depend on the Spirit of God to guide me. My meditation on these verses is my prayer for this kind of love. It is also a way of opening myself to the Spirit's guidance.

One of my children got a summer job at a service station about three miles from our home. Since we were a one-car family I knew we were in trouble. So together with my wife I decided to confront the problem early. While some young people might consider walking this distance, I knew *this* young person would not. I suggested to him that we buy a bicycle.

"It'll be our bike," I said, "for I would like to ride it also. But it will be for your use for transportation to your summer job."

He acted like he hadn't heard me. Later I tried again and this time he responded. "Go get a bike if you want one."

"You misunderstand," I said, "I want it to be *our* bike and I want your input on the selection." I almost had to push him into the car to go to the bike shop.

As we looked over the bikes, I would ask, "What do you think of this one?" "Get it if you want it," he would reply.

After a few such responses I decided to act. "Okay, we'll take this 10-speed," I said.

As we were tying it to the top of the car I said to myself, *This has got to be faced!*

As we got into the car I said, "Do you know what is on top of this car? A bicycle. That bicycle is your transportation to and from work this summer!" There was no avoiding me now. "I don't want to ride a bike to work," he said.

That did it! Whatever patience I had been exercising was now gone. "Listen," I said, "you are going to ride the bike. You are *not* going to tie up the car all day, and neither your mother nor I intend to be your chauffeur. That's it. Period!" He responded with sullen silence.

I am not good at dealing with sullen silence. I react instinctively by becoming sullenly silent myself. So on the way home we were both sullenly silent. When we arrived he got out of the car and slammed the door. I thought to myself, *I can slam it as hard as you!* And I did!

As I entered my study I was banging my fist into the palm of my other hand muttering to myself, "We've got to remain firm with these kids; we're too permissive."

As I was reinforcing my position with these mutterings, I heard something coming from deep inside me saying, *Love does not insist on its own way.* My first reaction was to say, "Shut up!" But the words would not shut up. I had meditated on them too long. So I said, "Lord, it doesn't apply!" That even sounded phony to *me*.

So I finally said, "OK, Lord, I'll listen."

Just then my son came into the study, obviously bristling with anger. "You never listen to anyone, do you?" he charged. I found this a rather uncomfortable accusation since I am supposed to be a counselor. "Did you ask me why I didn't want to ride the bike?" he asked heatedly.

"No," I admitted, "I guess I didn't."

"I'll tell you why," he said. "The county road that I have to travel on is a drag strip at night, and I don't get off work until 11 P.M. It's just not safe! So I'll make you a deal. I'll ride the bike to work and I'll try to get a friend to bring me home. But if at times I can't get a ride and you just happen to be around . . . would you mind coming to get me?"

I stretched out my hand. "You've got yourself a deal," I said. He stared at me. "What happened to you?" he said.

Should I tell him? A better question is, should I be honest? "The plain truth," I said, "is that the Lord got to me before you did."

I hate to think of the brouhaha that would have ensued if I had not heard the prayer of my heart at that moment.

Christ is formed in us

By meditating on the Word, the Word becomes a part of us. It is a practical way of participating in the process of "Christ being formed in us" (Gal. 4:19). For Christ is the living Word. His Spirit comes to us through the written Word. As we listen, repeatedly, the Word becomes an internalized influence in the shaping of our behavior.

In meditating on my prayer of the heart I had reconditioned myself to behave differently in this instance. Otherwise I could have written the script that I would have automatically followed. When my son accused me of not asking him why he didn't want to ride the bike I would have reacted by saying, "No, and I don't want to know. I don't care what the reason is; you are not taking the car and I am not driving you!"

You can use your imagination to deduce how he would have reacted to this authoritarian response. The chances are that with much volume and intensity we would have escalated the angry exchange until only sullen silence would have ended it once again.

Through repeatedly exposing ourselves to specific influences we can reshape ourselves to some degree. We can always revert to the prior conditioning, however. We are creatures of habit and old habits die hard. But as we do things differently we initiate the process of creating a new habit. Each repetition of the new reinforces its hold on us.

In choosing our own conditioning or reconditioning we are not only exercising our freedom, but also our responsibility under God. In the Christian context this choice is our response to the call of God to *grow*. The goal of our growth is described in the Scripture as "mature [person]hood," also defined as "the measure of the stature of the fulness of Christ" (Eph. 4:13).

15

Overcoming
Fear of Self

A by-product of meditation is that it helps us overcome our fear of ourselves. We humans tend to be uneasy with our own presence. This is the motivation for much of our chronic busyness. We involve ourselves in many activities and our busyness defends us against being alone with ourselves with nothing occupying our attention. We are more afraid of nothing than of something. We are afraid of an empty mind. "Idleness," we say, "is the devil's workshop."

What do we fear about being alone and unoccupied? Our inner demons? Our vulnerability to feelings we cannot direct? Rage? Panic? Despair? Loss of control?

A time for not doing

While meditation is something we do, paradoxically it is also something we *don't* do. It is a way to cease doing.

Meditation is a time for receiving, for silence, for listening, for being still and quiet in the presence of God.

We are not alone, even though we are by ourselves. We are really never alone. It is just that we think we are. We are always in the position for being in communion with God.

Our need for control over our inner life is met through this communion as we trust instead in God's control. The demons we fear are our isolation, our alienation, our rejection, our abandonment. These conditions are mitigated when we know who is God.

The gospel is the bridge between God's presence and our own. We are afraid of ourselves often for good reason. There are things about us we do not like. Getting close to ourselves brings these things to our awareness. If we are repelled by some of our thoughts, fantasies, attitudes, memories, words, and actions, how much more would the God of righteousness be repelled?

But God is *not* repelled. In an old and familiar phrase, we are "justified while yet sinners." We are loved while yet unlovable. We are forgiven while yet unreformed. We are accepted while still unacceptable. This is the good news; we can live positively with who we are—with our imperfections, our sins, our shadowy side, because God can live positively with us.

The practice of meditation helps us to feel at home with ourselves—or as Nouwen puts it, "to feel at home in our own house." When in our silence we listen to Someone, our fear of nothing—the empty mind—is overcome. God is here. God belongs with us. We feel at ease then in both presences—God's and ours.

From fear to serenity

God's presence brings us to peace with our own presence. The gospel of who God is is really the gospel of what God does.

God is not just love but a loving God whose love is shown in loving actions. God reached out to us—not just with a hand—but with the bloody hand of Christ. This is why the cross is the symbol of the Christian faith.

This is also why a lighted cross used as a Christmas decoration was removed by court order from a county courthouse in Mississippi. The cross is not just a symbol of religious faith but of the Christian faith. So its presence at the Mississippi courthouse was viewed as the government's recognition of a specific religion.

So let the lighted cross be moved to the church, where there need be no apology for a specific faith.

Christians believe, in a way that can only be conveyed by metaphors, that God was in the Christ of the cross reconciling a fallen world to God. All of the pain, the injustice, the cruelty, that stem from our alienation from our identity as God's people were experienced on that cross. Here is a love that will never let us go, that replaces the fear of ourselves, that provides security even in the darkness of the night.

It is our awareness of the presence of this God that devotional meditation helps us cultivate. In the presence of *this* God who is for us and who loves us, we can feel good about ourselves even when we disappoint ourselves. We do not have to justify ourselves to remain in God's presence. God has done that for us.

When through meditation we lose our fear of ourselves we move toward serenity—a healthy condition of spirit that brings health also to mind and body.

Part Three

Meditation as a Discipline that Acknowledges Feelings

16

Developing the Discipline for Meditation

The word *discipline* has received bad press. It conjures up images of overly-strict parents, of punishment, compulsiveness, legalism, and rigidity. All of these images are caricatures of discipline and do not portray discipline as it really is.

The word *discipline* comes from the New Testament word for "learning." The word *disciple* is from the same root and means "learner." As we learn from our experiences we accumulate wisdom concerning how we wish to live. Discipline means using our freedom as human beings to direct ourselves according to this wisdom.

Securing the motivation

When we are not clear regarding our priorities we lack the motivation for discipline. So the first step toward developing a discipline is deciding how we want to live our lives. Speaking from a Christian perspective, this means determining how we perceive God's call to us in order to establish priorities.

Once we know what we want, we can *learn* how to achieve it. But if we are double-minded or ambivalent about our priorities, we will have trouble living according to them. We need to examine ourselves for any resistance to our accepted priorities. Once we bring this resistance to the surface, we can make a rational decision about what to do with it. We will need to say *no* to the resistance and become single-minded toward our priorities.

You have the power to direct yourself according to your priorities once you have dealt with any resistance you may have toward them. This power goes with our freedom to respond to God's call in the shaping of our lives. But there are external as well as internal obstacles to exercising this freedom.

One such obstacle is the busy schedule in which most of us live. It can become so packed that if we introduce something new into it we have to remove something old. We need to use our power of choice.

But at times it may seem we have no choice. Young parents, for example, may long for the time to meditate, but between being parents, maintaining a home, and establishing a career, they can hardly "keep their heads above water" as it is. Yet if they *could* find time for meditation, their efforts in these other areas would benefit from this break in their schedules. But where will the time come from?

What I *don't* want to do is lay a guilt trip on anybody for not having time for prayer and meditation. If your motivation for meditating is guilt oriented, you will simply be creating additional resistance. For every "you should" that hangs heavy upon you, there is a compensatory "I won't" generated within you. This is why discipline is an exercise in freedom. When we feel coerced by guilt or fear into a discipline, our unconscious resistance to coercion will sabotage our efforts. This resistance is the only way we can exercise our freedom when we function under coercion.

So if you really don't see any time in your demanding schedule for meditation, know that God speaks to you also through your other activities. God speaks through your parenting, your work, and all the other activities of your busy day. You will need to be open to receive, to listen, so that you will "see" and "hear" what God is communicating. Meditation will make you more sensitive as a listener, but when this is not possible you can still listen in your other activities by reminding yourself that God is present.

The fact remains, however, that all of us need a break in our schedules—a time for centering, for focusing—and meditation provides this. If we go too long without such breaks, we will lose our perspective and become off-centered in our priorities. When we are off-centered we cast a shadow, and the shadow inevitably falls on our relationships.

If you really desire the opportunity for meditation you have taken the first step toward having it. Once you are determined to have it you will be open to possibilities. Remind yourself that developing a discipline is using your freedom to direct yourself, rather than allowing yourself to sabotage your best interests.

When you are ready

If you are open to the possibility of a spiritual discipline in the midst of your busy life, the *first* step toward this end is to know when *not* to meditate. In your demanding schedule of meeting other people's needs, the time for meditation is not when these others need you.

I had to learn this the hard way. I had developed my discipline of prayer when I was single. It took several years into marriage and family for me to realize that meditation time had no priority over marital and family obligations. Meditation had to wait when these obligations called, and God could speak more clearly to me through them than were I to neglect them for meditation. St. Theresa, who treasured her times alone with God in prayer, said, "When someone needs me, my prayers are over."

Knowing when not to meditate prepares us for the *second* step, which is when *to* meditate. The time selected should be the time most free from other obligations. As much as possible use the same time each day. In establishing a discipline this regularity of time is very important.

For most of us—even those in the busiest times of their lives—early morning is usually the best. Not only is it a time most free from interruptions, it is also a strategic time for setting the tone for the day. If we center ourselves in prayer before God in the morning, we are more likely to continue in this centered position throughout the day.

Some, of course, are not "morning" people. They come alive later in the day and reach their peak in the evening. If you are one of these, you will probably be wiser to look for a "hole" somewhere later in the day or in the evening.

The *third* step in the development of a discipline is to set a time limit for your meditation. Since devotional meditation depends on mental focusing, there are times when we can do this better than at other times. When our mind wanders easily, meditation could take longer if we desire to complete a specific format. Therefore, it is wise to determine a time limit beforehand. We will discuss this problem of mind-wandering later.

The *fourth* and final step is to select a place. While you may not have much choice, depending upon the cramped-ness of your living or work quarters, choose the place most conducive to an attitude of worship. The surroundings are important for this attitude, as the designers of worship ed-ifices know. Again, it is important to the discipline to use this same place each day if possible.

Formation of a habit

Developing a discipline is establishing a particular kind of habit. Like all habits, it is harder to do it in the beginning stages than later when it is established in one's life-style. Resistance to the habit will show itself mostly in the begin-ning stages. So keep at it. The longer you do, the less the resistance will trouble you. Soon the habit that you "take yourself in hand" to establish will be something you look forward to doing.

At first, the press of time, fluctuating interest, interrup-tions, and mood swings may all conspire to thwart your efforts. There is a point in the process, however, a "con-tinental divide," at which the momentum will begin to shift in the opposite direction. Your natural resistance to what is new will begin to diminish as the new begins to form its own habit tracks. What was formerly an opposing inertia has now shifted to your side.

In developing a discipline, however, one still needs to be free when the discipline has become a habit. We need to exercise this freedom when confronted with a choice be-tween competing interests for our time, even our meditation time. In such choices we may exercise our freedom under God *not* to meditate. Meditation is a God-given support and not a law-oriented compulsion. Should a day go by when we have chosen to give our meditation time to some other priority, we need feel no guilt. For our own sakes, however, we may not want to omit our meditation time very often, since we will miss the enjoyment of the experience and also its centering influence.

Redeeming the time

As we mature in this life we become increasingly aware of the value of time. "It goes so fast!" "Where did it go?" Consequently, we would not want to *waste* any of it. We are most likely to do this when we are confronted with unanticipated blocks of time in which there is "nothing to do." We *wait* in line, in traffic, or are put on hold on the phone, or endure the breakdown of services in airports or in our homes. The New Testament has the intriguing phrase, "redeeming the time" (KJV). How can we redeem the time in these waiting times rather than wasting or "killing" it? Whether it is five minutes, twenty minutes or an hour or more, we can utilize these times for meditation.

When we do, we not only redeem the time, but are treating ourselves kindly as well. We tend to stress and frustrate ourselves during these unexpected delays. The energy generated by impatience is often destructive. Even boredom is a form of anxiety. Meditation reduces all of these stresses and in their stead encourages serenity.

We can utilize these waiting times for meditation if we don't let our resentment over our inconvenience or our irritation toward those responsible for the delay get to us. Anger and resentment can frustrate our attempts to focus our minds. While our delays may well be due to the carelessness and inconsiderateness of others, if we allow our resentment toward them to consume the waiting time, we have given these persons even more power to frustrate us. Since time is precious, it is to our enlightened self-interest not to let this happen. Patience rather than impatience is needed to redeem the time.

17

Patience in Discipline

Henri Nouwen defines patience as looking to the present moment rather than to the future for our purpose, meaning, satisfaction. The present moment is all the time that we actually *have;* so we need to make the most of it.

Since the present moment may not be that attractive—in fact, may even be painful—we need patience to redeem it. It is significant that the word *patience* comes from the Latin *pati* meaning "to suffer." In redeeming even painful times, we are allowing God to speak through them so that we continue, even then, to be those who are open to God's blessing, to be *receivers*.

When our minds wander

One of the chronic problems requiring patience in meditation is the penchant of our minds to wander rather than focus. Several factors may account for those times. One is our mood swings. If I am excited about something positive or disturbed about something negative, for example, my mind seems to be claimed by these emotions. Also when I am overly tired I find it difficult to focus. You may discover other influences that create the same problem for you.

At these times we need to be patient with ourselves and tolerant of our wandering minds rather than becoming discouraged. We are always able to return our mind to that which we desire to focus upon once we are aware that it has wandered. We never lose this ability regardless of how often we have to do it. As we persist in returning our mind we are learning to take charge of it. This also is a discipline and through our persistence we will grow in our self-control.

Creative stimulation

There are times also when our mind is stimulated by something in our meditation and takes off on its own. I have found these are often beneficial digressions which become part of that particular meditation. Since the meditation has a predetermined time limit, we need not feel tension over being "behind" because of these digressions. Meditation is not something to accomplish. We are not trying to become good meditators. We can screen out these achievement-oriented goals of our culture when meditating. There is nothing to prove—nothing to "become good at"—nothing to "get finished." We are not *trying* to do *anything*—but to be open and to listen.

So if you need help in stopping before you are really "finished," use a timer. During times when I am emotionally disturbed I allot a certain amount of time to each of the distinctive parts of my meditative pattern. When the time allotment is up I move to the next part even though I may not have completed the previous part.

Knowing that we have a limited time has a "Parkinson's Law" effect on us. (The amount of time it takes to do something is determined by the amount of time allotted to do it.) We are more apt to use the time as we had planned than if the time limit were open-ended.

Drowsiness

Another problem we may encounter in meditation is drowsiness. Our mind wants to wander into sleep. This may occur simply because we are tired or because prayer and meditation are relaxing. When we are beginning our disciplinary development, drowsiness may also be a way of escaping. We may not yet be at ease with the silence of our own presence. New endeavors create their own tension. We are not familiar enough to feel secure in what we are doing. So we easily slip into doing what we usually do when alone with ourselves in a relaxed position; we go to sleep.

Since drowsiness is encouraged by our relaxed physical position in meditating, changing the position may help. Instead of lying down or even sitting, try meditating while standing or walking. The rhythm of walking may even help our meditation. In fact, the discipline of "taking a walk" or even running can be combined with meditation. I know from experience that meditation while walking or running enhances my satisfaction with both of these activities. Since we cannot escape by drowsiness while walking or running, we can grow accustomed instead to this meditative focus.

Beyond patience

Although we always have the power to return our mind to our meditative focus once we realize it has wandered, we may not be able to keep it there. Our feelings are too intense. Our sense of self-control is overwhelmed by them. When this is the case we may not even realize that our mind has wandered until a sizeable piece of time has gone by. It is time then to go beyond patience to wisdom. Should you find yourself emotionally preoccupied you need to move from prayer as meditation to other forms of prayer—prayer as catharsis or prayer as praise—depending on which feelings have taken charge of you.

18

Dealing with Disturbing Feelings

Meditation depends on our capacity for focusing our mind. In the anxious approach to life so common to our culture, our minds move at a frenetic pace in several directions at once. A friend in this situation who really desired to meditate, after many attempts finally concluded that meditation was beyond her. "I simply can't slow my mind down enough to do it," she said.

Behind the agitated mind are disturbed feelings. Before my friend and others like her can focus their minds, they need to deal with their feelings. She had trouble meditating because her rapidly moving mind had become a habitual way of life.

Others have this condition *occasionally*, producing the problem in meditation of the wandering mind which we discussed in the previous chapter. These also will find it better to focus first on their feelings when they find it difficult to meditate—in order to restore their capacity to focus their minds to meditate.

If you have either a habitual or occasional difficulty in slowing your mind and find that your ability to focus is inadequate to the task, then move beyond your thoughts and ask what it is you are *feeling*. Before you can engage in prayer as meditation, you may need to engage in prayer as catharsis.

Let it out to God

When we are too emotionally upset to focus our minds we need to express to God how we feel. Let it out! This kind of prayer could mean shouting or wailing. It is the way of becoming able again to listen—to receive.

Perhaps you are reluctant to express to God such disturbing feelings, as well as the thoughts that accompany them. What you would hear if you did may not sound like a good Christian or a devoted believer. What is to be gained, you may ask, in making such a verbal spectacle of oneself before God?

You need to ask yourself what is to be gained in *not* letting it out to God. God knows what is going on inside of us whether we put words to it or not. We are not enlightening God by putting words to our feelings. Rather we are sharing what God already knows—but what *we* need to express when we are aware of God's presence.

I mentioned the value to me on occasion of praying aloud—not for God's sake but for *mine*. So in like manner putting words to our disturbed feelings in the presence of God is good for *us*. It is a biblical way of coping healthily with these feelings.

Not a nice way of praying

Some may find it strange to conceive of this kind of communication as prayer. It is anything but the serene surrender of those who are at peace with themselves and God.

Perhaps we have been influenced too much by the mystics in our understanding of prayer and not enough by the biblical psalmists. Some of these psalmists' prayers are so violent in language that we hesitate to use them in public worship. "Break thou the arm of the wicked and evildoer; seek out his wickedness till thou find none" (Ps. 10:15).

Some of us are "nicer" than our biblical models. John, for example, had persistent difficulties with a couple of contentious persons with whom he works. He tried hard to get along with them, but the more he tried the more critical they became toward him. Because he was a sensitive person he suffered a great deal over these relationships.

Through his religious beliefs John discovered a way of dealing with the problem. "I've found that it helps if I pray for these persons," he said. "I seem to have a better attitude toward them when I do."

I asked John if he had ever shared with God his feelings about these people and also his thoughts of what he would like to do to them in retaliation.

John looked puzzled when I asked this and also like he had been caught. "No," he said blandly, "I haven't."

Praying for those coworkers helped John resolve his bad feelings toward them because the prayers changed his perspective of them. God changes us through prayer. God may also have influenced their attitude toward him through his intercessions. God changes things through prayer. But because John did not deal directly with his bad feelings toward them he engaged in a form of denial. He did not see that feelings are a normal part of our humanness. These feelings are bad only because they make him feel bad and not because they are bad in themselves.

His prayers, then, were not completely honest since he had not shared these feelings with God.

By bypassing this direct approach to his feelings John had

missed out on the therapeutic potential of such sharing. As helpful as his prayers of intercession were, they would have been even more helpful if he had also put words to his feelings of resentment.

He may have felt like fantasizing about getting even with those coworkers who offended him: telling them off, snubbing them, or quitting as a way of hitting back.

Since we share the fallenness of humanity these emotional reactions come naturally. But we assume they are not acceptable to God. Therefore we do not deem them acceptable to the language of prayer. So then what happens? Either we keep this part of our person from God—and feel subliminally guilty about it—or we try to repress it—and hope it goes away.

In either case the feelings remain and influence our behavior in negative ways. When we repress our feelings or keep them separated from our prayer life, it is not because we are too Christian to soil ourselves in God's eyes. It is because we are not Christian enough to believe that what is unspoken is still known to God—that putting words to our feelings reveals nothing that God does not already know. The question then is not whether God knows but whether God accepts.

19

Acceptance through Forgiveness

What is acceptable to God? *I* am! *You* are! Does this include our feelings of anger and panic and depression—with all of the retaliative and childish and doubting thoughts that go with them? Of course—they are part of us! Our feelings are included in our bonding of acceptance. Our Baptism is the seal of this bonding.

The bonding holds

Like any other problem in our relationships, our disturbing feelings are more likely to be resolved when we bring them out in the open than if we conceal them. If we bring them out in the open with God by putting words to them in prayer, we are less likely to act out on them. As violent as the psalmists sounded, they were less likely to act violently after letting it out. Their catharsis while conscious of God's presence was therapeutic.

Our Baptism covenant is still in effect in such letting go. The Christian understanding of acceptance is based upon divine forgiveness. It is distinct from our various cultural understandings of acceptance. In spite of our violent feelings we are secure in the unconditional love of God. It isn't that there are no conditions. There are! But God has met them for us. This is why Christian acceptance has the cross at its center.

Even as our Baptism is the sign of our bonding with God, the Lord's Supper reaffirms this bond. As in our relationships with people, we need also to be told we are loved by God even though we know it. In the Lord's Supper with its appeal to the senses, God reaches out to touch us and remind us that we are loved and cared for.

Why is it healing to let our feelings out to God? Again, because of the cross. Christ is the "Lamb of God." He is the offering—the sacrifice. Through Christ God removed the conditions—the *thou shalls* and the *thou shall nots*—so that despite our violent feelings our relationship with God would have no conditions other than God's love.

God as Jesus

Yet in the paradox of our faith, Christ is not only the Lamb and sacrifice of God; he is also the revealer of God. I find it helps to think of God as Jesus when I wonder how God can possibly accept me when I express emotions of hate and hurt and anger.

This was the mental image of God that the psalmists had. Otherwise they would not have had the temerity to let go in God's presence. Of course, they didn't know the historical Jesus of Nazareth, but they knew the God who was in Jesus "reconciling the world to himself" (2 Cor. 5:19).

Those who suppress their feelings in order to be good

Christians are unliberated by the gospel to be who they are. They are more influenced by the period of the Enlightenment, when human reason was exalted over the chaos of emotion, than by the ideal of humanity in Jesus. They are more influenced by the image of irenic sainthood than by our biblical models—Elijah and Jeremiah in the Old Testament, Paul the apostle and particularly Jesus in the New Testament—who were often anything but irenic in their passions.

When we exclude our volatile feelings from our prayers we are engaged in the anachronism of attempting to impress God—to create a favorable image of ourselves in God's mind! Can you imagine anything more ironic? How can you impress a God who knows everything about you and who accepts you by grace alone?

20

Liberated to Be
Who We Are

Lament in God's presence when you feel down. Cry when you feel sorrow or despair. Shout when you are angered, even enraged, at an injustice. Wail when you feel lost and panicky. Grieve over your losses. Voice the gnawing protest—Why? Put words to your disappointment over your unfulfilled hopes. Express how deflated you feel when you have experienced a rejection. And if you hold God accountable for some of these reversals—or for at least not preventing them—tell God so.

A model for "letting it out"

No matter how accusative you become in God's presence, you will have a hard time surpassing Job, who put God into the terrifying role of an enemy warrior.

All was well with me, but he [God] shattered me;
he seized me by the neck and crushed me.

He has made me his target; his archers surround me.
Without pity, he pierces my kidneys and spills my gall on
    the ground.
Again and again he bursts upon me;
he rushes at me like a warrior.

                                                (Job 16:12-14)

How could the New Testament letter of James refer to
Job as steadfast or patient when he talks like this about his
lot? (James 5:11).

It was by quarreling with God over what had happened
to him that Job was able to hold steadfast to his faith. In
fact, his openness to God about his feelings was an act of
faith. He believed that God could take it—and take *him*.
Although it may sound like Job is planning to abandon his
devotion to God, he is really engaging in a lover's quarrel.
He is quarreling in order to preserve his devotion.

Jesus—whom psychoanalyst Carl G. Jung says is God's
answer to the quarreling Job—actually became another Job.
Amidst the abandonment and horrifying pain of the cross,
he used the words of the psalmist to cry out, "My God, my
God, why hast thou forsaken me?" (Mark 15:34 from Ps.
22:1). Did that mean he was abandoning his faith? Far from
it. For he committed his spirit into the hands of the very
God whom he accused of forsaking him.

Obviously these outbursts against God were the sufferers'
way of holding to their faith. They were communicating
how they felt to the God who seemed to have abandoned
or even attacked them. Henri Nouwen described these lover's quarrels with God as the movement from protest to
prayer (*Reaching Out* [Doubleday, 1966] pp. 93-94). Actually the protest *is* prayer. The movement then is from
prayer as protest to prayer as meditation.

Letting out our disturbed feelings in the presence of God

is a way of moving away from those feelings. My experience is that I can let myself feel sorry for myself in God's presence—not as a way of staying there, but as a way of moving out of this mood. To do this does not spoil God's image of me. I can retrogress to the level of a child in God's presence as a way of moving genuinely—from within—to the level of an adult. God knows me better than I know myself. As the apostle Paul says, my goal is to "understand fully, even as I have been fully understood" (1 Cor. 13:12).

God as parent and counselor

God is not threatened by our questioning or even attacking God's guidance. God has no fragile ego like we mortals have. The Almighty is not upset by our apparent disintegration into a crying child or disappointed in our choice of words to communicate, as many people who care about us would. So be a child in God's presence when that's the way you feel and let the Heavenly Parent accept you as you are.

Our "critical parent" image of the divine needs to be replaced by the "nurturing parent" image. Let the nurturing Parent cuddle your wailing child. It is comforting to know that you don't have to keep strong for God.

Gail had never grieved openly over the death of her father, although she was deeply wounded by the loss, because, in her words, she had to "be the shoulder for the others in the family." She resented this role but felt unable to put it aside. In God's presence Gail can abandon it and say rather than just think the shocking fantasies of her mind.

By expressing how you really feel in your prayers you will be helped to meet your adult challenges in the world. You will be strengthened in this way as Jesus was, even if it means being strengthened to endure a cross.

No guilt over therapy

We need not feel guilty over such retrogressions in God's presence. We who are justified in God's eyes by God's grace have nothing to prove with God. We don't have to keep up an image. No public relations program is needed or possible.

Rather we can see such catharsis in God's presence as our recognition of God's place in our life. God is our Heavenly Counselor and we experience the divine therapy.

Guilt over such behavior in prayer would be the result of thinking God is like us. We would be reducing the Heavenly Parent to our image of some earthly parents. We are not trying to make an impression—"How am I doing, God?"—but rather we are using God's means for making genuine changes within ourselves. If we realize this, whenever we are surprised by the maturity and wisdom of our actions our reaction will not be "God must be proud of me," but rather, "Thank you, God, for getting through to me."

This is the therapeutic way of emoting—of getting our feelings under control through healthy expression rather than a compulsive suppression. In a culture which has neglected the care of emotions, it is difficult to perceive this paradox: genuine control of feelings comes through a healthy expression of them. Through cathartic prayer we deal with our feelings and restore our capacity to focus our minds so that we can return to prayer as meditation.

21

Dealing with Feelings of Elation

We can also find it next to impossible to meditate when we are elated. We are simply too excited to focus.

When elated with good feelings, as when we are upset by bad feelings, we need first to let the feelings out to God. Express them as praise. Hallelujah! We can scarcely conceive of *hallelujah*, which means "praise the Lord" in Hebrew, being said in a flat voice. When the praise comes spontaneously we are too full of feelings to say it blandly. We either shout it or sing it.

Again it is the psalmists who show us the way to express our feelings. "Clap your hands, all peoples! Shout to God with loud songs of joy!" (Ps. 47:1).

A soaring passion

As with bad feelings, letting go with good feelings to God is therapeutic. The familiar problem for the atheist—whom to thank when filled with gratitude—is a serious one for human health. The believer has an open channel. Direct your deep sense of gratitude to God the giver. Eulogize, praise the goodness of God. Express the gratefulness from deep within your soul. "O give thanks to the Lord, for he is good" (Ps. 136:1).

Human joy is a soaring passion. It reaches for the transcendent. It needs to be expressed in praise to God. The Christian perception of the joy of life is *joy in the Lord*. Its most repeated praise expression in the Scripture is, "Sing to the Lord a new song" (Ps. 96:1). Charles Wesley captured the passion in his glorious hymn:

> *Oh, for a thousand tongues to sing*
> *   My great Redeemer's praise,*
> *The glories of my God and King,*
> *   The triumphs of his grace!*
>
> *The name of Jesus charms our fears*
> *   And bids our sorrows cease,*
> *Sings music in the sinner's ears,*
> *   Brings life and health and peace.*
>
> *To God all glory, praise, and love*
> *   Be now and ever giv'n,*
> *By saints below and saints above,*
> *   The Church in earth and heav'n.*

Let it out

It is healthy to feel joy, to let go with it, to let it out to God, to shout, to sing. Music seems often the only fitting way to express our joy. The "Hallelujah Chorus" in Handel's *Messiah* is the epitome of this expression in the Western world. Who can hear it without feeling it? It brings goose bumps, even tears. The receivers respond to the joy of the music. When the chorus comes, they stand. They've stood ever since King George III stood when hearing the premier performance of the *Messiah*.

Some say George stood at this point because he was simply tired of sitting—or to relieve his hemorrhoid pressure. Who knows? But I seriously doubt if the custom would have continued through the centuries if those who continued to hear were not moved to give the same expression to their feelings. We need to stand! Standing is a symbolic movement toward the transcendent. The chorus transcends the ear—"King of kings and Lord of lords!"

When our good feelings excite us we want to praise the God of grace. Not only are lover's quarrels passionate, lover's delights are also. In our human relationships lover's quarrels can lead to lover's delights. So also in our relationship with God. Quarrels that are honest though passionate expressions of feelings can lead to reconciliation when these feelings are accepted.

Reconciliations are joyful occasions. They move us to celebrate, to praise, to worship, to give glory to God. God is the original Reconciler, and all reconciliations are ultimately reflections of God's grace.

Praise is the liberated response of a receiver of grace. "Worthy art thou, our Lord and God, to receive glory and honor and power" (Rev. 4:11). This response can reach ecstacy on occasion. Then we need to express it as holistically as possible—by shouting, singing, and dancing.

Dancing is the expression that includes the body. It also has its role in the Bible as an expression of joy. At harvest time women celebrated by dancing. They were jubilant over the fruits of the earth that would provide life for them and their families. They also danced when the men returned safely from battle. Dancing also was a way of praising the Lord. "Let them praise his name with dancing" (Ps. 149:3).

David's dance before the Lord as he brought the people's symbol of their worship, the ark of the Lord, to Jerusalem was an ecstacy of joy. "And David danced before the Lord with all his might" (2 Sam. 6:14).

When our perspective is conditioned to see the reality of grace in all of God's doings, we have a greater appreciation for living. We see the "whole giftedness and wonder of life," smelling the flowers, appreciating people, praising God, loving people, loving God. This is the perspective on life that draws from the present moment all of its potential for joy. Because we are open to receive, we receive more, and because we receive more, we are more grateful. In our meditation we can help to shape this perspective by our use of imagery that conditions it.

So when you are too excited with joy or enthusiasm to meditate, prayer as meditation needs to give way to prayer as praise. Let out the joy to the Lord in whatever form seems to express it best for you—sing, shout, dance, or weep. Hallelujah! When the excitement subsides there is opportunity again for meditation.

22

Congruity
with Feelings

The psalms are passionate with lament and anger; they are also passionate with joy. Some of these psalms—which biblical scholars call psalms of the individual—often begin with an expression of disturbing feelings and conclude with an expression of positive feelings. As the psalmists expressed their negative feelings, their feelings changed. They began then to express confidence and hope and finally praise.

The normality of ups and downs

By dealing directly with their feelings when they felt bad and when they felt good, the psalmists showed they were aware of—and accepted—the up and down nature of human emotions. In contrast, some of us may lose this awareness when we are either in our up or down.

When we are down it may seem that we shall never be up, and when we are up we can be under the illusion we will never again be down. By using the psalms in our meditation we will help ourselves keep our feet on the ground when we are up and keep our head in the air when we are down.

Letting out our feelings to God when we are down may actually initiate the change for better feelings. A change in mood often takes place, for example, midway through a psalm of lament. The change begins with the words, "but thou."

A case in point is Psalm 22, the psalm which Jesus cried out from the cross in his despair: "My God, my God, why hast thou forsaken me?" (v. 1). Midway through this psalm a change in mood begins with the words: "But thou, O Lord, be not far off! O thou my help, hasten to my aid!" (v. 19). At this point the psalmist becomes liberated to recall the positive times of life. God was helpful to me in the past; God will be helpful to me now.

If we communicate our emotions to God when we are disturbed—"God, I'm angry; I'm depressed; I'm raging"— we are beginning the process of viewing our lives, at least to some extent, in a more positive way. Directing our feelings to God even when we quarrel with God takes the blinders from our eyes and old landmarks of faith come back into view. Then we can take the leap of faith that this renewed perspective has made possible.

Unsnagging ourselves

We may not always experience a change in our perspective when we let out our feelings to God as depicted in some of the psalms. As I am sure you are aware, you can get stuck in the downs—mired in the focus on the negative.

Should this occur you will need to dislodge this focus by directing yourself to the specific parts of your meditation pattern that provide you with pictures of hope (described in the next chapter). After you have meditated for a period of time, certain favorite verses or images will come to mind. In this way your are asserting your desire to move from the hold that your negative feelings have over you. You are making the attempt to unsnag yourself so that you can move to the good feelings implicit in your pictures of hope.

I find it helpful to "see" Christ calling me to move in this direction.

The threat of joy

But there may be more to our resistance to move than a temporary miring down in the negative. Joy itself is a problem for some people. They believe, possibly subconsciously, they don't deserve to be joyful. They stifle their joy.

Such persons have a need to show God—or the universe—they are sorrowing over their sinfulness so God—or the universe—will be aware they are not receiving more benefits than they deserve. Otherwise, if they allow themselves to be happy, God—or the universe—will see that they are not suffering sufficiently for their unworthiness and will let something bad happen to them to rectify things. "Don't laugh too hard," as the old aphorism goes, "or you'll soon be crying."

What I have been describing is a grace-less mentality. It can creep into our minds even when we know better. We don't see very much grace in the world around us and we may be influenced more by this influence than by our Christian faith. For our Christian faith is in direct contrast to this mindset. We are liberated through our faith to face reality—including our emotional reality. When things happen to us that make us feel good we can allow ourselves to be joyful.

This is an appropriate response to reality—to accept and extol it.

The fear of anarchy

The way we interpret what we see and hear influences the generation within us of either negative or positive feelings. As we have noted, it is possible some may interpret life negatively because they cannot tolerate joy. If they could change their perspective of themselves, they could see and hear the pleasurable. Others interpret life positively because they cannot tolerate sadness or depression. This means they repress their awareness of the negative even as others repress their awareness of the positive.

Yet people who have problems accepting either positive or negative feelings find it difficult to tolerate feelings per se. In screening out particular feelings they find threatening, they end up screening out all feelings. They defend themselves against passion. For them passions are uncontrollable and chaotic. Their defensive mindset is their way of staying in control—but at a terrible price to their humanity.

Psychotherapist Ann Wilson Schaef believes we get into this bind quite naturally since our institutions—families, schools, churches—tend to "prepare us to fit into a society where 'frozen feelings' are the norm" (*The Disease of Co-Dependency* [Minneapolis: Winston Press, 1986] p. 69).

When we fear our feelings we are actually fearing ourselves, for our feelings provide us with information about ourselves. In this instance it would be information we don't want to receive. In our fear of passion we prefer the tyranny of suppression to the anarchy of expression. Having a need for a tight rein over our own passions we also feel we must extend this rein over the passions of others.

Liberated for living

It is from this bind—this ever-spiraling retreat from life—that the gospel liberates us. In being liberated to be who we are we can affirm our own creation. God created us as persons not only with intellect and will but also with feelings. We are liberated both to feel and to express these feelings.

Feelings provide us with vitality. They are signs of our genuineness—the source of our animation. But feelings fluctuate. Some days we are full of them and other days we seem depleted of them. Our response to the happenings of our day to day living has much to do with this fluctuation as does the replaying of tapes within us. Changes in our biochemistry also contribute to this fluctuation.

We can thank God for our feelings. Whether comfortable or uncomfortable, they are expressions of our caring, consequences of our involvement in living, and the beating of our spiritual pulse. We need to treat them respectfully and to express them healthily.

Part Four

Meditation as a Structure of Tradition and Innovation

23

A Guided
Meditation

Having described meditation, I would like now to lead you in meditation. We need to involve ourselves in meditation to understand what it is. In this chapter I will provide a step by step guide to follow. In line with the holistic emphasis of meditation, the first step is the relaxing of your body as a way of relaxing your mind and opening your spirit to the Spirit of God.

I suggest you read the guided meditation before using it. This will give you an idea of what is involved so that you will be prepared for the guided steps.

You may want also to tape the guided meditation and use the tape of your own voice. Then you can listen without the distraction of reading. The tape, however, as well as the guide itself should serve only as a helpful structure until you work out a meditation pattern of your own. Some parts of this meditation you may want to keep while subtracting others and adding some of your own. You will find that your meditation format will evolve continually and will become distinctly yours.

If you decide to tape the meditation, read the instructions into the recorder and time the silences between steps as indicated.

The meditation will take approximately 20 minutes. When you have this amount of time relatively secured against interruption I suggest you sit in a hard chair. Besides being good for your back, you can tell when you are relaxed on a hard chair when it feels like you are sitting on a cushion. In a soft chair you will never know. Sit straight in the chair (really the most comfortable position) and put both feet on the floor.

Rest your arms on your thighs.

Shut your eyes to keep out distraction and to protect your inward focus. As temples of the Holy Spirit we can conceive of ourselves as having within us a shrine which we enter for meditation. Envision this shrine in whatever way you find helpful.

Guided meditation

Begin by relaxing your toes. Drop each toe as though it would go through the floor. Let go until you can't let go anymore (*10 seconds*).

Now move to the calf muscles of your legs. "See" your muscles as they really are—fibers sheathed together; see these fibers in your calf muscles relaxing and becoming loose and flexible (*10 seconds*).

Now do the same with the thigh muscles of your legs. "See" these muscles letting go and becoming loose (*10 seconds*).

Let your hips sink into the chair. Let the chair hold you up. Relax your back muscles, beginning at your hips and moving toward your shoulders. See these muscles becoming flexible—unspasmed. Tell them to become loose. Feel them let go *(20 seconds)*.

When you reach your shoulders go to your fingers and drop each finger as you did your toes—letting go of each until all of the tension is released *(10 seconds)*.

Now move to your forearm muscles and "see" them relaxing as you did the calf muscles in your legs *(10 seconds)*.

Then go to your upper arm muscles—feel them let go. Tell them to be at ease *(10 seconds)*.

Slowly and very carefully rotate your neck above your shoulders, first in one direction and then in the other—and then let your head balance itself on your neck *(10 seconds)*.

Drop your lower jaw. When we are tense we tend to clench our teeth. When we are relaxed our teeth probably will not be touching *(10 seconds)*.

Relax your facial muscles—tell them to let go *(10 seconds)*.

Now from the top of your head to the bottom of your feet, feel the ease of your body at ease—and feel how good that feels *(10 seconds)*.

While you are feeling the goodness of this ease, listen to these words from the letter to the Romans that also make us feel good. "For I am sure that neither death, nor life, nor angels, nor principalities, nor things present, nor things to come, nor powers, nor height, nor depth, nor anything else in all creation, will be able to separate us from the love of God in Christ Jesus our Lord" (Rom. 8:38-39) *(10 seconds)*.

In the quiet we become aware of sounds and actions that otherwise would not register on our consciousness such as our breathing. As you become conscious of your breathing, take a deep breath of air from your diaphragm and breathe out. Do it again and catch the relaxing rhythm of your breathing *(10 seconds)*.

Recalling that the biblical word for *breath* and for *spirit* is the same, as you inhale think of taking in the Holy Breath, the Holy Spirit, and let the Holy Spirit cast out the disruptive and obstructive spirits from within you. If you know what some of these poisons are, see them leaving as you exhale *(10 seconds)*.

In the peaceful repose between your exhaling and inhaling, hear these words from the old covenant: "Be still, [that is, be comforted, be secure] and know that I am God" (Ps. 46:10) *(10 seconds)*.

Focus now on your abdomen. Let your exhalation take you there. Think of your abdomen as the biblical symbol of your compassion and affection. "See" your intimate family members and friends for whom you feel affection, and feel this affection from the abdominal region. "See" yourself embrace each of them *(20 seconds)*.

Now think of the people for whom you feel compassion—friends or family members who are physically ill, others who are emotionally unstable or who are having marital or family trouble, persons who are chemically dependent or who are unemployed. Choose one of these for this meditation. Let yourself feel your compassion for this person from your abdomen. "The beginning of healing," says Henri Nouwen, "is in the solidarity with the pain" *(Reaching Out,* p. 43) *(5 seconds)*.

Now take the leap of faith and "see" this person healed—in whatever way healing may mean for them. Dare to "see" it—this is your prayer of intercession for this person. So inwardly in your heart say amen to it *(10 seconds)*.

One symbol for God in both Old and New Testaments is *rock*. "Lead thou me to the rock that is higher than I" (Ps. 61:2b). Picture Jesus' parable of the house built on the rock (Matt. 7:24-27). "See" the wind and rain of the storm lash against the house on the rock but it does not fall *(5 seconds)*.

But Jesus' parable is about people. So "see" *yourself* standing on the rock. Whatever storms may be blowing in your life, let them blow. You will not be blown off because you are on the good foundation. You may want to get down on your hands and knees or lie flat on the rock, but you will not be blown off *(5 seconds)*. If others are participants with you in these storms have them join you on the rock *(5 seconds)*. As you "see" yourself firm on the rock in the midst of the storm, hear these words from Proverbs: "Trust in the Lord with all your heart, and lean not on your own understanding. In all your ways acknowledge Him, and He shall direct your paths" (Prov. 3:5-6 NKJV) *(10 seconds)*.

I will close the meditation with a prayer of the church. Grant us, O Lord, for our spiritual growth, thoughts that pass into prayers, prayers that pass into love, and love that passes into eternal life. Through Jesus Christ our Lord, Amen *(end of taping)*.

Other options

This guided meditation may be expanded at several points.

The intercessions would normally include several persons for whom you have particular concern.

Prayers for your own illnesses and pains can be offered by the use of mental imagery directed to God. Picture the area of your body that is ailing and "see" your disease-resisting antibodies bringing healing to it. Then envision yourself healed. Since this "seeing" is directed to God, include the inward amen. If you can familiarize yourself with the physiology and anatomy involved in the illness and healing process, incorporate this knowledge into your imagery of meditation.

Another option that helps me reaffirm God's unconditional love for me and gives me hope for self-improvement is the imagery of the mirrors. I will describe it in the guided meditation format in the event you want to tape it.

Imagine a mirror with a blue frame. This is the mirror of *reality*. Look into it and "see" yourself as you really are. "See" the things about you that you like—and the things about you that you don't like. As you dare to "see" as much of yourself as you are aware, remind yourself that this is the self that God loves. "I have loved you with an everlasting love," says the Lord, "therefore I have continued my faithfulness to you" (Jer. 31:3) *(10 seconds)*.

Let God love you as you are. "See" the "arms" of God coming from the cross of Christ and embracing you—not just your good parts, but all of you, your total person *(10 seconds)*.

After this embrace of God, "see" yourself putting your own arms around yourself, your total self *(10 seconds)*.

Now "see" yourself put your arms around someone you find difficult to love *(10 seconds)*. "Love your neighbor as yourself" (Matt. 22:39) *(5 seconds)*. "We love, because [God] first loved us" (1 John 4:19) *(5 seconds)*.

Now picture a mirror with a silver frame. This is the mirror of your *becoming*—the mirror reflecting what God can do with those who are forgiven in Christ. The apostle Paul writes, "The fruit of the Spirit is love, joy, peace, patience, kindness, goodness, faithfulness, gentleness, self-control" (Gal. 5:22-23) *(10 seconds)*.

Look into the mirror of becoming and dare to see yourself with these fruits. "See" yourself, loving, patient, and kind

(10 seconds). Since this is also a prayer for these fruits, direct this picture to God as you "see" yourself receiving what God wants to give. Say the inward amen to it *(10 seconds)*.

We as well as I

In closing the guided meditation with a prayer of the church I was tapping into a rich source of prayers—namely those from the traditions of the church.

The value of these prayers of the church (frequently called *collects*) is not only that they are beautifully worded and universally applicable in their petitions, but that they are almost always corporate. They follow the example of our Lord's prayer in which one prays as *we* and *us*. In teaching us to pray in the plural Jesus joined prayers for oneself and for others in a corporate understanding of human life.

The prayers of the church use the plural because they frequently are prayed with others in worship, and because of the interdependent nature of the Christian fellowship. Each member of the body is praying not only for himself or herself but also for other members so that the whole body can function properly because "each part is working properly" (Eph. 4:16).

The petitions of these prayers are phrased in general terms so each person can interpret them in personal as well as universal imagery. The personal is like the species within the genus or larger family. As psychotherapist Carl Rogers put it, "What is most personal is most universal."

The universal character of the petitions permits their use through the centuries. The implication is that we who pray them will place them within the context of our own era and personal situations.

When our children were young I was inspired by an authority on prayers of the church who encouraged families to memorize the prayers that spoke to their personal and family needs. So our family took on the task of memorizing several prayers; an example follows:

> O God, from whom come all holy desires, all good counsels and all just works; Give to us, your servants, that peace which the world cannot give, that our hearts may be set to obey your commandments, and also that we being defended from the fear of our enemies, may live in peace and quietness, through the merits of Jesus Christ our Savior, who lives and reigns with you and the Holy Spirit, God forever.

I am impressed by the wisdom implicit in this as well as others of these old prayers. For example, we do not pray for deliverance from our enemies, but from the *fear* of our enemies. The real enemy is actually within us—our fear. How can we love our enemies as Jesus directed us while we yet fear them?

The value of memorizing these prayers is that we have them in our heads when we need them. Their petitions can be used in meditation like the prayer of the heart (see page 69). The same is true for the memorization of Bible verses, which frequently—as with the psalms—are prayers themselves or at least can be used as prayers.

In conclusion

Devotional meditation is one way of using the means through which God is revealed that God has given us. It is a way of sharpening the sensitivities of our faith to perceive God's presence when some of our other sensitivities only perceive God's absence. Our awareness of God's presence in trying times may make the difference between a response of trust or a response of desperation and panic.

The effects of the discipline of devotional meditation tend to be cumulative. Usually the effects are gradual so that one becomes aware of them only after one has ceased to anticipate them. Yet change is taking place. The thoughts and images we meditate upon come to mind more and more when they are needed. This has its healthy effect on our behavior—both inwardly and outwardly.

These thoughts and images bring with them their association with the Presence of God. This awareness diminishes our defensiveness—What is there to defend?—and makes us more open and sensitive to the people with whom we are involved. Then we can hear God speak to us through them.

Epilog

Soaked in
the Scriptures

One of the disadvantages in the many translations we have of the Bible is we have ceased to commit to memory those passages that speak to us in our needs. I was introduced by my pastor to the practice of memorizing Bible passages, prayers, and hymns as a young teen. The value of this practice motivated me to do the same for the children I instructed as a parish pastor.

This practice has all but disappeared from church education programs. Yet there are sufficient testimonies to its value that I hope we return to it.

Kathryn Koob, one of the Iranian hostages, paid tribute to her church training for providing her with the Bible "in her head" when her captors refused her one. She shared her memories with her cellmate on a daily basis and together they were spiritually strengthened by them during those long and difficult days of captivity.

Theologian Joseph Sittler describes himself as "soaked in the Scriptures" from his home environment. "Time and again," says Sittler, "phrases come back when you need them. The ancient vigor, color, sonority, of the language of Scripture has a kind of stickiness to the memory. Phrases remain like forgotten deposits in an account; but they are there for resurrection" (*Gravity and Grace* [Minneapolis: Augsburg, 1986] p. 46).

One of the fears we have about aging is memory loss. Should this happen we are more likely to recall religious memories rather than others. Memorized prayers and scriptural passages are likely to stay with us even when other mental facilities are ceasing to function.

Though memorization is not valued at present, it remains a valuable asset in the enhancement of our prayer life—and a particular asset to prayer as meditation.

As you grow through the Word in your relationship with God, new insights into yourself, your work, your relationships, as well as into God's influence in your life, will evolve. These are brought to our awareness by the widening scope of the Light that en*light*ens us. We are the objects of the Creator's continuing creative activity, as through Christ God continuously shapes us as his *new creation*.

It is helpful to record these insights and enlightenments in a journal. As I am shown by the guidance of God where I need reinforcement for my new conditioning, where I need to let go of control, where I need to trust, to *see* God's healing activity, to believe where I am inclined to doubt, I describe these enlightenments in my journal.

Often these insights come from my frustrations and failures or even regressions into old ways. But it also helps to describe our successes and victories when the Holy Spirit got through to us where often we have resisted this guidance.

Writing things down has a way of fixing them in our minds. It also gives a sense of completion or closure on an experience, freeing us to enter anew into the next moment.

Also we can reread our jottings and see the activities in our lives in which God has guided us.

I wish you God's blessings as you live your life of faith using the means God has provided. I hope your times of meditation and prayer will provide you with the orientation you need to meet life's challenges creatively. "Soaked in the Scriptures," we can continue to celebrate God's comforting presence.